The Crusade of Ramon Llull

The Crusade of Ramon Llull

Evangelism and Apologetics in the Thirteenth Century

NUMA GOMEZ

WIPF & STOCK · Eugene, Oregon

THE CRUSADE OF RAMON LLULL
Evangelism and Apologetics in the Thirteenth Century

Copyright © 2022 Numa Gomez. All rights reserved. Except for brief quotations in critical publications or reviews, no part of this book may be reproduced in any manner without prior written permission from the publisher. Write: Permissions, Wipf and Stock Publishers, 199 W. 8th Ave., Suite 3, Eugene, OR 97401.

Wipf & Stock
An Imprint of Wipf and Stock Publishers
199 W. 8th Ave., Suite 3
Eugene, OR 97401

www.wipfandstock.com

PAPERBACK ISBN: 978-1-6667-4497-2
HARDCOVER ISBN: 978-1-6667-4498-9
EBOOK ISBN: 978-1-6667-4499-6

09/15/22

CONTENTS

Preface		vii
1	Introduction	1
2	Historical Context	13
3	Theology and Philosophy of Ministry	26
4	Apologetics and Averroes	40
5	Apologetics to Jews	57
6	Apologetics to the Culture	70
7	Evangelism, Discipleship, and Impact on Society	85
8	Concluding Thoughts	99
Abstract		109
Bibliography		111

PREFACE

BEFORE YOU IS THE dissertation "The Crusade of Ramon Lull: Apologetics and Evangelism to Muslims during the Thirteenth Century," the basis of which is an example of the usefulness and necessity of apologetics in evangelism and missions work. It has been written to fulfill the graduation requirements for the Degree of Doctor of Philosophy of The Southern Baptist Theological Seminary (SBTS). I was engaged in researching and writing this dissertation from May 2015 to April 2017.

April, 2022

1

INTRODUCTION

Ramon Llull or Raymundo Llull, was a thirteenth-century Dominican monk who lived during a tumultuous period in Spain's history. He was born in Catalonia, which was an independent state until Spain annexed the Catalan plain during Spanish expansion. In 1212, the armies of the three main kingdoms, Aragon, Castile, and Navarre, overthrew Muslim rule that had governed Spain for some three hundred years. Spain became a Christian kingdom and expansion gained inertia and strength through the military might of the King of Aragon, James II. The fighting between Muslim and Christians continued until the fourteenth century, or about 1343. Born into a wealthy and influential family, Raymond Llull became a Knight of the Crusades, during the last of the crusades, around 1232. He had a conversion experience around the age of 28, and became the foremost evangelist and missionary to Muslims. Those who have studied missions believe Llull is the first and greatest missionary to Muslims.[1] He is also recognized as the greatest Catalan mystic and poet whose writings helped influence Neo-Platonic mysticism throughout medieval and seventeenth-century Europe.[2]

EARLY LIFE

Llull's early life was lived as a profligate youth. He was worldly and, though he was married at twenty-two and had several children, was quite the "ladies' man." However, after his conversion to the faith, it is said he loved

1. Zwemer, *Ramon LLull: First Missionary to Moslems*, 5–7.
2. Bonner, *Doctor Illuminatus*, 9–12.

Christ with a passionate love. He believed love for Christ and love for the lost should be the only motivating factor to evangelize and teach the lost. Llull also spoke out against some of the doctrines of the Catholic Church (this period is pre-Luther). The Catholic Church labeled him a heretic and excommunicated him in 1376, sixty plus years after his death. Nevertheless, many modern missionaries and historians believe Llull understood salvation by grace in the blood of Jesus Christ.[3] Llull knew nothing but the Catholic Church and was always in good standing during his life. Llull's basic aim in his writings and ministry was the conversion of Muslim and Jews, or as he often put it, "that in the whole world there may not be more than one language, one belief, and one faith."[4]

The benefits of the Crusades, minimal as they were, were being felt in Spain, France, and Italy during Llull's days. Life and morality of the Middle Ages had disparate contrasts. There was inspiring faith along with degrading superstition. It was a time of self-denying altruism to suffering Christians, to barbarous cruelty to infidels, Jews, and heretics.[5] Wealthy Christians paid huge ransoms to redeem Christians who were enslaved by Muslim captors, yet also paid hefty sums to persecute those who erred from the faith. During this time, there were great popes and priests who were reformers, yet both the papacy and the priesthood were rife with corruption. It is in this period that Llull came to faith, then began serving and living for the Lord.

There are a couple of stories of how he came to the faith. One story, and probably the more credible one, is that Llull had a series of visions while he was still carousing and living a worldly life. In one vision, while writing a somewhat licentious love song or poem to a woman (not his wife), he saw Christ on the cross. This vision unsettled him, but he continued on, until about a week later when he saw the same vision. After receiving these frightful visions four or five times, he concluded, after a full night of prayer, that God was calling him to leave his sinful life behind and follow Christ. He also concluded after some time that he should reach out to the Saracens (Muslims), who surrounded Christians on all sides, inspired by the writings and actions of St. Francis of Assisi who lived earlier, and had reached out to the Muslim community in hopes of converting many to Christianity.[6]

---

3. Johnston, *Evangelical Rhetoric of Ramon Llull*, 3–10.
4. Cross and Livingstone, *Oxford Dictionary of the Christian Church*, 996.
5. Zwemer, *Ramon Llull*, 14.
6. Bonner, *Doctor Illuminatus*, 12–14.

MISSIONARY INTEREST

Llull eventually became a monk and joined the order of the Dominicans, but later tried to join the Franciscan order because they were more willing to work in the outreach to Muslims. Llull had joined the Dominicans primarily because of geography. There was a Dominican monastery in his homeland and they were receptive to Llull's vision of evangelism and training of other evangelists to reach Muslims. However, when Llull encountered obstacles in setting up these training centers, the Dominican order advised he not push, since the papacy was undergoing a tumultuous time and there were more pressing matters. Llull found more sympathy and cooperation for his cause from the Franciscans, and tried to change from the Dominican to the Franciscan orders, but was denied. In fact, he was threatened with excommunication if he changed orders, so this ended the matter officially. Unofficially, Llull continued to work with Franciscans in outreach to Muslims, while remaining in the Dominican order. Given that the only other "missionary spirit" of the twelfth and thirteen centuries was that of the Crusaders, Llull's work was unique and emphasized the true work of Christ.[7] Llull set out to prove what the Crusades could have accomplished if they had been fought with the cross instead of the sword. Llull mastered the Arabic language and conceived a new idea for reaching not only Muslims, but Jews and pagans as well. This idea was named the *Ars inveniendi veritatem*, later changed to just *Ars generalis*.[8]

Llull's missionary spirit fueled his apologetic focus as he set up the first training center for lay missionaries in Majorca, then Paris. He taught Arabic, which he had learned earlier from a slave under his care and ownership. His decision to target Muslims with Christian philosophy and fully explain the Trinity to them sets him apart from anyone else of his time. In 1300–01, he preached to Majorca's Muslims and wrote several books about not only his experiences, but also his devotion to Christ. Llull's objective was to unify the three Abrahamic faiths under the banner of Christ. Personal revelation and mysticism were not only important components of his philosophy as well as the reason for his writing and debating in Arabic, it also fueled his poetry and prose.

---

7. Bridger, "Raymond Llull: Medieval Theologian," 1–4.
8. Lohr, "The New Logic of Ramon Llull," 24–25.

LLULL THE APOLOGIST

Llull's apologetic work focused on refuting the philosophy of the Muslim philosopher Averroes. Llull's purpose was to show the "Mohammedans" (a common term in that day to refer to Muslims) the error of this philosophy so much so that they could not fail to see the truth. The strength of the Muslim religion, in the age of scholasticism, was its philosophy. With this in mind, Llull developed a system or "logical machine" if you will, where theological propositions could be arranged in circles, squares, triangles, and other geometric figures so as to show themselves true. It was a device whereby opponents could not outright reject his arguments. Llull lived in a time where Muslim and Christian lived together after Spanish Christians subdued Muslim rule, but the country remained very much a multicultural region. With Jews, Muslims, and Christians living together, apologetics was difficult since the three monotheistic religions had similar views on morality and topics such as ethics, eternal life, soul studies, etc. Llull's device helped illustrate the holes in his opponents' arguments. Llull held that, unlike what Muslim philosophers taught about the division of philosophy and theology, there was no distinction between those two disciplines.

Llull held strongly that even the highest mysteries could be proved by means of logical demonstration and the use of the *Ars Magna*, a shorter version of his greater work, *Ars Generalis Ultima*. This belief was the foundation of his philosophy and theology, which he called his Art (*Ars* was the standard scholastic translation of the Greek τέχνη or "craft"). Much of the Art is an anthology of various writings to which he added and explained their effectiveness. Llull's *Generalis Ultima* tried to make logical deductions in a mechanical instead of a mental way. It was an early means of producing knowledge. Some people speculate this may have been a rudimentary device of what is known today as a computer.[9] It is generally assumed that this method influenced later mathematics such as Gottfried Leibniz and Marin Mersenne.[10] Though this method did not win many converts, it is a step in the advancement of computations and computation theory.[11]

The foundations for Llull's great Art for discovering the truth was a series of nine virtues or "divine dignities." These attributes or virtues were interrelated. Every attribute, when combined with another, affirmed an important tenet of the Catholic faith. The English translations of these virtues or attributes are goodness, greatness, eternity or duration, power, wisdom,

---

9. Vega, *Ramon LLull and the Secret of Life*, 56–59.
10. Wilson, "Early European Mathematics," 82.
11. Montgomery, "Computer Origins and the Defense of the Faith," 189–90.

will, virtue, truth, and glory. They all serve the purpose of demonstrating the "correlation of philosophical or scientific knowledge with Christian doctrine."[12] When combined with another, these essential attributes display or explain who God is and/or demonstrate the logic at arriving at a conclusion of who God is. Combining these virtues, like goodness and greatness, or goodness and power, greatness and eternity, etc., led the believer into the deeper knowledge of the Godhead. These letters, displayed in a circle with the letter A at the center, connect these virtues and represent the combinations they can form.[13]. Figure 1 depicts how one arrives at truth whether it be for private spiritual formation and meditation, apologetics and evangelism, and scriptural exegesis. It helps guide the believer in spiritual truths. Many have said this only served as a mnemonic device and was not of much use otherwise. It was Llull's hope through his Art that Christians would win the Saracens (a generic term for Muslims during Llull's era and throughout the medieval era[14]) for the cause of Christ.

Llull set this chart up in part to oppose the philosophy of Averroes. During this time, Averroist philosophy opposed reason to faith. Llull attempted to show these two were reconcilable and intricately related. He tried to show Muslim philosophers that the real opposition to faith was agnosticism and not logic.[15] Llull believed that the weakness of Islamic theology fell on two points: lack of love coming from their God, Allah; and lack of harmony of Allah's attributes. These beliefs along with his Art were the strong arguments that, in his opinion, would convert many Mohammedans. Llull held that wisdom would point to the truth that true religion should ascribe to a God perfection, both moral and aesthetic.[16] Any religion that could not acknowledge the principles in his Art was deficient or defective.

---

12. Johnston, *Evangelical Rhetoric*, 13–14. Johnston suggests that Llull substitutes these virtues by using letters of the alphabet, B, C, D, E, F, G, H, AND I respectively. The letter A is used for symbolizing all the absolute principles of the Godhead. The other letters symbolize absolute virtues of the Godhead. This chart, drawn in a circle with A in the middle, symbolizes God is a single essence with multiple attributes.

13. Vega, *Ramon LLull and the Secret of Life*, 62.

14. Zwemer, *Ramon LLull*, 35.

15. Zwemer, *Ramon LLull*, 40.

16. Zwemer, *Ramon LLull*, 44.

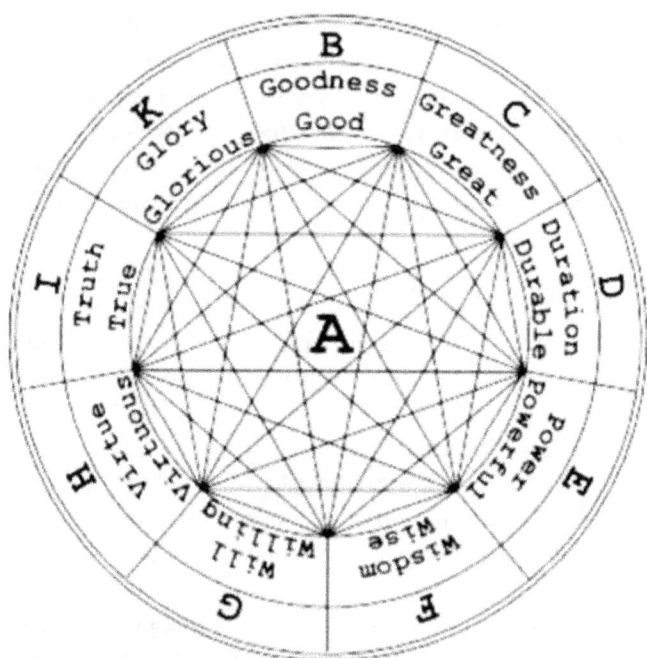

Figure 1. Divine dignities

In Averroes' belief in the separation of reason and faith, he recognized that truth comes from these two distinct yet equally authoritative sources, which often led to some apparent incompatible claims. For instance, there was the claim of the eternity of the world, derived from philosophic argumentation, versus the created universe, which comes from Scripture. Averroes believed that scripture (Qur'an) proposed rather than prohibited the study of philosophy. Yet, philosophical claims are different from revealed claims. Further, Llull would argue that these claims must be proven by "demonstrative reasoning," while Scripture claims are true because they are revealed in Scripture to be so.[17] Seldom did Muslim philosophers use any demonstrative reasoning to justify their philosophic claims since these might contradict religious claims of faith. Averroes asserted that one could not ascertain religious truths from philosophic reasoning.[18] Averroes also spiritualized Aristotle's view of creation, which was not the biblical concept

17. Buijs, "Religion and Philosophy in Maimonides, Averroes, and Aquinas," 161–62.

18. Buijs, "Religion and Philosophy in Maimonides, Averroes, and Aquinas, 163–64.

of creation, but was a theory of origin that should not be confused with the Genesis account. Llull exposed this weakness, or at least tried to demonstrate the faulty reasoning of this particular Muslim philosophy, through his Art.

In his works, Llull exalted the doctrine of the Trinity as central to evangelism, spiritual formation, and apologetic work.[19] Llull also felt personal testimony was far superior to any philosophic argument because it testified to the power of the gospel and not to a system. His Art was used as further proof of the Muslims' faulty reasoning concerning the Almighty God. Averroes again interpreted Aristotle's "immovable mover" as God yet did not go as far as the biblical text to distinguish God as a personality.[20] Llull believed only Christianity satisfies or possesses what other religions lacked. And this Art was only a method for proving the articles of the Catholic faith. He used those qualities that all three Abrahamic faiths could agree on but still prove those unique qualities the Christian faith could claim, such as the Trinity, the incarnation, and resurrection.[21] There is a strong connection between the Art and Aristotelian topics being discussed during the Middle Ages. During the twelfth century, Aristotle's philosophy was rediscovered by the West. Muslim philosophy translated much of Aristotle's writings in Arabic and much of the success of Muslim advancement was due in part to the Greeks, particularly Aristotle.[22]

Llull's Art was not only an attempt to refute Muslim philosophy, but also to prove the Christian mysteries of the Trinity and the incarnation. Other theologians and clerics, such as Raymond of Peñafort, Thomas Aquinas, and Ramon Martí, had tried before to argue this (with Muslims and Jews) but had failed. Llull knew that appealing to authority of Scripture was pointless since foes had their scriptures to counter, so he needed another type of proof to explain these mysteries. He also took into account faith and reason that was acceptable (in terms of belief) to all three religions, as well as other considerations such as Semitic origins and Greek influence.[23]

APOLOGETIC METHOD

In light of this apologetic method, this work investigates how effective his apologetic work was to his culture and time. The thesis of this work is that

19. Lohr, "New Logic of Ramon Llull," 27.
20. Averroes, *Theology and Philosophy of Averroes*, 13–20.
21. Bonner, *Art and Logic of Ramon Llull*, 13–15.
22. Rubenstein, *Aristotle's Children*, 14–15.
23. Bonner, *Doctor Illuminatus*, 48–50.

though Llull did not convert many Muslims, his method is valid because in Muslim culture in his day, as it is today, reason and logic play an important role in the Muslim faith. Llull understood that arguing from religious texts was futile, but given Islam's belief in God speaking through the cosmos, Llull believed reason and logic was an open door for refuting Muslim belief. Even modern Muslims believe that in order to understand and confirm the truth of Quranic signs, they need to "keep an eye" on the cosmic signs, i.e. on things and events, and if one wants to comprehend the cosmic signs one should "keep an ear" on the Qur'an. In other words, humans are to observe the universe while listening to the Qur'an and vice versa, for just as the universe is the Creator's speech through deed, the Qur'an is his speech through word.[24] It is also important to realize that Muhammad, who was the author and first teacher of the Qur'an, taught that God speaks to everybody, at all times, through the Qur'an. According to the Qur'an, man knows intuitively that there must be a Creator and he understands what the Creator is, but in order to know Him, he needs revelation. Muslim scholar Ibn 'Arabi (1165–1240) explains that only through rational means can one acquire the knowledge of the existence of God and of what God is not.[25] This rational thought led Muslims to minimize God's role in the daily life of the believer and gave more emphasis on philosophy and acts of the individual Muslim for salvation. Llull's Art set out to prove how Muslim philosophy minimizes God's role in salvation, including how Islam teaches that God has the ultimate say as to who is to be saved.

In addition, Llull believed his Art was a useful tool for evangelism. Samuel Zwemer has described Llull as one whose "faith was not sacramental but personal and vital."[26] He chose to reach out specifically to Muslims because the Christian world did not love Muslims in the thirteenth century nor did they understand their religion. However, he believed the Christian faith answered all rational objections whether from Muslims or pagans. His Art could be used as a superior source of knowledge about God that, upon hearing it, would convince many to come to Christ. His scholastic philosophy was elevated by a fiery zeal for the spread of the gospel. One may dismiss his Art as just a series of circles and tables, but one could not deny his passion for reaching the lost. He felt if one presented a rational view of Christianity before the lost, it would convince many unbelievers to convert.[27] Zeal

---

24. Corduan, *Neighboring Faiths*, 99–102.

25. Kars, "Two Modes of Unsaying in the Early Thirteenth Century Islamic Lands," 261–78.

26. Zwemer, *Ramon LLull*, 48.

27. Zwemer, *Ramon LLull*, 34.

for reaching the Muslims drove him to start Arabic training centers. He started his first training center in Majorca, then Paris, then later throughout southern Europe, and his Art would convince many, so he thought, of the truths of the Bible over any writing. He entreated various popes to establish other training centers for this work as well. Llull's Art could also be used to show how those characteristics of God display God's love for his creation more so than any Muslim philosophy could demonstrate. Moreover, it was because of this great love that humanity could understand God better, and not be left cloaked in mystery. Llull's Art was often used in analogous ways to demonstrate this great love.[28]

The Art further shows that this apologetic tool was used for the inspiration and spiritual growth of believers who used it. The Art affirmed believers of those qualities of God needed for drawing closer to Him. They were a resource for great study and contemplation in the believer's life. After all, it was a resource for discovering the truth about any subject pertaining to the Godhead.[29] In addition to being an evangelist and apologist, Llull is considered the "John Bunyan" of the Catalan plain. He was a prolific writer on various topics, especially dealing with the inner life of the believer. He wrote at least 486 Treatises on theology, spirituality, and philosophy, but he is best remembered for the two Catalan classics, *The Book of the Lover and the Beloved*, and *Blanquerna*.[30]

LLULL THE EVANGELIST

Equally important, Llull was an evangelist with a heart for the Saracens.[31] Llull's most important apologetic work includes *The Book of the Gentile and the Three Wise Men* and *Blanquerna*. Llull's success, however, hinged on the ability to demonstrate that the Christian faith was the truth because it provided rational evidence to bolster its claims. Llull refuted Averroes' claim of

---

28. Bonner, *Doctor Illuminatus*, 51–53.
29. Johnston, *Evangelical Rhetoric*, 13–14.
30. Bonner, *Ramon LLull: A Contemporary Life*, 7–14.
31. Claudia Valenzuela, "Faith of the Saracens," 311–30. In the Middle Ages, this was a reference to any person–Arab, Turk, or other–who professed the religion of Islam. Earlier in the Roman world, there had been references to Saracens (Greek: Sarakenoi) by late classical authors in the first three centuries after Christ, the term being then applied to an Arab tribe living in the Sinai Peninsula. In the following centuries, the use of the term by Christians was extended to cover Arab tribes in general; and, after the establishment of the caliphate, the Byzantines referred to all Muslim subjects of the caliph as Saracens. Through the Byzantines and the crusaders, the name spread into western Europe, where it was long in general use and has survived until modern times.

"double knowledge," arguing that both theology and philosophy were compatible and not two separate sets of truth. Averroes did not believe these two were in conflict, just that they were different ways of reaching the same truth. Averroes also believed in an eternal universe and that the human soul was composed of two parts, one is part of the human (individual) and the other part was divine. Llull also grasped the features shared by the three religions and combined them to demonstrate that if someone understands these features well, it was sufficient to lead that person to the Trinity and the Incarnation. Llull believed that theology was best understood in the context of missionary enterprise.[32]

The inference to be drawn here is that Llull's work emphasized glorifying God and refuting false beliefs about God. He spoke of virtue while speaking and promoting Christian truth, and being "in love" with God was far above all other loves. To do this, Llull glorified God above all other gods and he not only exemplified these virtues in his life, but he struggled to teach others to do the same. Llull was responsible for setting up training centers in France, Italy, and Spain to teach the Arabic language for the purpose of missionary enterprise to Muslims. Nevertheless, he did not neglect the beauty he saw in both Christ and Christianity. Llull has been compared to Roger Bacon, in his strong belief and teaching of complete scientific education for missionaries.[33] Yet it was not just his intellectual ability that made him a great missionary, but it was an ardent devotion to his Lord and the church. Llull reached out to the Saracens even though there was an increasingly hostile atmosphere between Christian and Muslim. The increasing spread of Christianity and its theological growth created a new hatred between adherents of both faiths.

Llull ventured into the mission field, taking the gospel to Muslim lands in Africa and Syria. He carried on the work of St. Francis of Assisi who started the evangelism of Muslims earlier in the thirteenth century. This, in part, led to his favoring the Franciscan Order over the one he had already committed to, the Dominican. He boldly went and proclaimed Christ to Sultans and Muslim leaders. He made several trips to Africa, and he suffered incarceration and physical violence for his faith. It is believed that he died on a return trip from one of these trips. Llull had been beaten and jailed for speaking of the Trinity and the Incarnation. He fell ill in large part because of his age; he was past the age of seventy. It was on the return trip to Spain that the great apologist died.

---

32. Montgomery, "Computer Origins and the Defense of the Faith," 18.
33. Barber, *Raymond Llull: The Illuminated Doctor*, 8.

LLULL THE MYSTIC

As mentioned, Llull worked closely with the Franciscan order though he originally joined the Dominican order, but was not formally allowed to leave the order for another. However, he found a more receptive audience to his spirituality and brotherly support from the Franciscans, as St. Francis had a great influence on this order that bears his name. Llull produced more than two hundred and sixty works on various topics. He wrote poetry and mystical works. As mentioned, he is considered the Catalonian "John Bunyan," writing such titles as *The Book of Lover and the Beloved* and the *Art of Contemplation*. As a mystic, Llull wrote about the Divine perfections and focused on the contemplation of these. In *Book of the Lover and the Beloved*, Llull revealed a richness and simplicity in these meditations as if to imitate the Song of Solomon in its display of love for the beloved, the "one every heart yearns for."[34] He believed that if the believer concentrated on the lovely attributes mentioned in this work, through memory, understanding, and will, it would result on the believer bringing greater glory to God as well as bringing purification while giving wisdom to the believer.

The thirteenth and fourteenth centuries were the age of Franciscan spirituality. Francis of Assisi had influenced those who sought a deeper inner life. Determined to walk in the footsteps of Christ, Francis rejected worldly pursuits for a life of devotion and poverty. This injected a new life and theme into the discourse of religious life. Francis celebrated nature and no longer believed that the Cathedral was the only sacred place, but found divine fingerprints everywhere, including nature.[35] This spirituality influenced many and was continued by Llull. Llull was a strong believer in the beauty that glorifies God. Llull was one of the first Europeans to write religious stories and poems in the vernacular. But always, evangelism was behind his writings. His life was full of romance and adventure and so was his writings. He spoke of a beauty that came through language and poetry, and imitation (of Christ's character), eloquence, and order. Llull was a mystic, and explored the mystical life. He felt that many did not understand the mystical life and that the general population had no use for mysticism, deeming it unpractical. He also felt that in order to reach a state of union with God, one must be "as a fool" in his relations with the world.[36] He considered himself a disciple of St. Francis of Assisi. Yet, he never lived a cloistered life. His life was full of exploration and excitement in the service of his

---

34. Peers, *Art of Contemplation*, 82.
35. Robson, *Cambridge Companion to Francis of Assisi*, 3–5.
36. Ramon LLull, *Book of the Lover and the Beloved*, 1.

Master. Much of the language he wrote in reminds one of either the Song of Songs or even the *Pilgrim's Progress*. He was impressed by the writings and accounts of martyrs whose prayers and visions were recorded as having seen the glory of heaven and of the Lord. Llull longed for these types of visions, which may have been why he seemed to seek martyrdom.

In subsequent chapters, I explore Llull's spirituality and how it influenced not only his personal life, but also his apologetic and evangelistic work. It is good to start with Llull's spirituality and mystical writings since it is central to his faith and it influenced his missionary zeal and his apologetic work.

2

HISTORICAL CONTEXT

Ramon Llull lived in a tumultuous era, both politically and spiritually. His life intersected with that of St. Francis of Assisi, though it is doubtful the two ever met. Deep spirituality and contemplation marked the lives of both men, and though similarities exist in much of their thought and life, they also took very different approaches to ministry and evangelism. Both men tried to reform the medieval church and both had a living active faith that would be recognized as evangelical by modern standards. Francis was less political than Llull, that is, he did not appeal to church hierarchy or popes for favors to carry on his work in other lands, as he was more of a separatist, preferring a monastic life, separate from worldly pursuits and possessions. Llull was not afraid to entreat popes and to travel to establish training centers. He upset powers from time to time, but always for the cause of missions and evangelism, and not just for the sake of stirring things up.

SPANISH CULTURE AND SOCIETY

Sixteen years before Llull was born, St. Francis had courageously proclaimed the gospel to the Sultan in Damietta (Egypt). Francis, filled with a holy zeal, went uninvited and ready to give his life.[1] Such was the spirit of the age, filled with a few fearless souls willing to sacrifice all for Christ. There was a resurgence in the desire to be martyred for Christ from some willing individuals, as the monastic life often taught the value and significance of this ethic. It was not unusual for many who had a conversion experience and

---

1. Basetti-Sani, "Muhammad and St Francis," 247.

associated themselves with the monastic life to aspire to die for Christ. Missiologists Eugene Stock and Robert E. Speer believe that Llull was one of the greatest missionaries to Muslims because he valued this principle. Spanish history should be taken into account in understanding the spirit of this age. Through the centuries, Spain had seen invasion after invasion. During the fifth and sixth centuries, it was Catholics against Arians for control of the Spanish peninsula. Later, it was the Romans against Goths in this same struggle. By the end of the seventh century, it was under Muslim control. At Cordova, Muslims displayed their power and dominance of culture through architecture, sword casting, art and jewelry, poetry, philosophy, and medicine. It was during this flourishing of Islamic culture that Averroes reintroduces Aristotle to the west.[2] The reappearance of Aristotelian ideas had a transformative effect on both Muslim and European cultures. Aristotelian ideas would eventually turn Europe into the main catalyst of global civilization.[3] This is not to say that all Islam accepted the claims of philosophy. One of the most influential figures in philosophy during this time, Al-Ghazali, attacked Aristotle's philosophy in a book titled *The Incoherence of Philosophers*, which ended rationalistic thought in the Arab Muslim world. Though Averroes wrote and reintroduced Aristotelian thought back into Muslim Spain, he was later condemned and exiled.[4]

In this context, St. Francis would teach and display the virtues of Christianity, which influenced medieval spirituality for centuries. In the spirit of the age, Llull's spirituality was born and influenced in this cradle, as he later carried the mantle of evangelical theology. St. Francis reached out first to the Muslim world in love and compassion and with a deep-seated desire to save them with the gospel. In an era that saw the Inquisition and the Crusades, as well as the overthrow of Muslim rule from the Spanish peninsula and southern France, Francis was the apostle of love.[5] Francis' spirituality influenced many who were searching for more than just an existence. He explained the intricacies of the gospel in a striking and convincing manner. He related the gospel in such a way as to involve the entire person or being. Thomas of Celano stated, "Francis made a tongue of his whole body in service of Christianity."[6] This remark was a reference of Francis' persuasive manner in regard to preaching and teaching his brand of spirituality, using his entire being. When Pope Innocent III called for another Crusade to the

---

2. Barber, *Raymond Llull: The Illuminated Doctor*, 12–18.
3. Rubenstein, *Aristotle's Children*, 7–8.
4. Rubenstein, *Aristotle's Children*, 85–87.
5. Basetti-Sani, "Muhammad and St Francis," 248.
6. Robson, *Cambridge Companion to Francis of Assisi*, 34.

Holy Land to oust Muslim rule in 1215, Francis, unwilling to support war, sought peace between the warring parties and met with the Sultan of Egypt, al-Malik-al-Kamal. The Sultan listened to Francis as he saw the great saint was a man of peace and faith. The Sultan even asked for prayer from Francis so that he may know God's will in ruling and in the matter concerning war. It is not certain what Francis said to the Sultan, but what is known is that Francis spoke, and the Sultan listened.[7] Francis' high christological beliefs may have been at the center of the conversations; nevertheless, no one believes that this encounter is a model for inter-religious dialogue today. The discussions did not bring any converts but they did bring peace and Francis' reputation grew.

The beginning of the thirteenth century saw Christianity once again as the prominent religion of the Spanish peninsula as well as in southern Europe, but in reality, Muslim decay had begun back in the tenth century. The overthrow of Muslim rule and reestablishing of Christian rule by placing Christian nobles who had been loyal to James I of Aragon established the Llull family and other Catalan nobles. The Islands of Majorca, Minorca, and Iviza were firmly under Christian Catalan rule. It was at Majorca that Llull distinguished himself to King James I of Aragon. Llull was rewarded for his loyalty and bravery in fighting off Muslim rule in Majorca by becoming lord of certain territories in Palma and the vicinity thereof. Years earlier, Llull's parents desired that he receive an education in the arts and letters, but young Llull preferred freedom rather than education. His parents then secured training for him by the royal court in Majorca. He was a man of the public, admired for his chivalry as well as for his display of pleasure and carousing. As a young single man, Llull was a page in the royal court of Majorca, but lived a profligate life. His lifestyle caught the attention of the king. The king, displeased with Llull's routine, thought it best that he should marry. He was introduced to Blanca Picany and the couple married after a short courtship. Of course what Llull needed was reform and not marriage, and his dissolute life continued. Llull became a father to three children but this still did not prevent him from chasing the wives of other men.[8] In *Phantisticus*, Llull wrote that he had been "married and with children, reasonably well off, licentious, and worldly."[9]

The culture of Llull's early years was one most familiar to westerners; it was that of the troubadours, in which Catalan culture was saturated. The content of many of the troubadours' songs and sonnets were that of chivalry

---

7. Prior, "Francis of Assisi and a Cosmic Spirituality," 174–75.
8. Barber, *Raymond Llull*, 20.
9. Bonner, *Ramon LLull: A Contemporary Life*, 9–10.

and romantic love. The word *troubadour* is etymologically a masculine word; troubadours were mainly males. Many of their songs ranged from the metaphysical to comedic, intellectual to vulgar, rhetorical to formulaic. At this moment in history, the fruits of the conquest were being enjoyed by Spanish society; Muslim slaves (about a third of the population) and Jews (a small minority) played an important part in the economic and cultural life. A Muslim slave introduced Llull to the Arabic language. As a knight and a courtier, Llull would have traveled extensively through Aragon, Valencia, and Catalonia, which would be a larger classroom than any university could ever give him. It would earn him knowledge of the world.

CONVERSION AND SPIRITUAL FORMATION

In 1266, at the age of thirty, Llull experienced what most believe was a conversion to Christianity. There are a couple of stories about how he was converted. One of these stories is more probable. A conversion story that gets repeated often, but is dismissed even more frequently, tells of Llull setting his eyes on a beauty, a noble woman by the name of Signora Ambrosia di Castello of Genoa. Infatuated by her loveliness, Llull wrote many romantic sonnets to her to no avail. The noble woman discouraged Llull from writing any more sonnets and to stop pursuing this evil passion. Llull dismissed her gentle rejection and continued writing to her. It is further told that Llull, seeing her one day walking to her abode, was taken by her and rode up to her dwelling. The woman, seeing how such a desperate passion deserved a desperate wake up, allowed him to enter her chamber, where she revealed her nude upper torso.[10] The sight shocked, and even frightened Llull into a sober reality of, not the beauty of her breasts, but one breast consumed by cancer. This sight startled Llull, as did the words of the noble woman pointing to the folly of his ways and urging him to turn toward Christ. For several days, Llull lamented until he recovered and was able to give his life to the Lord.[11]

Many have excluded this story of his transformation, as details are difficult to corroborate. The story most associate with his actual conversion is that one evening in Majorca, while composing a "worthless song,"[12] Llull saw a vision of Christ on the cross as if it was suspended in mid-air. The

---

10. Peers, *Ramon Llull*, 3–4.
11. Barber, *Raymond Llull*, 20.
12. The term is Llull's usage for sonnets he wrote prior to his conversion. It may have been a vulgar song, but this was a way he referenced his work whether it was licentious or not. It was an expression of his work prior to his conversion.

vision disturbed him so much that he decided perhaps that he was sleep deprived and made his way to bed. A week later, about the same hour, he saw the Lord appear to him as in the previous visit. None of the first two visions kept Llull from practicing his licentious ways and on the following day, once again, saw this same vision, then again a few days after that. It was on either the fourth or fifth visitation of Christ on a cross that Llull, now terrified of these visions, tried to understand their significance. He concluded that these visions were pointing him to give his life to Jesus Christ, but he resisted because of the guilt he felt of his current life and past indiscretions.[13] He had a mixture of overwhelming guilt and understanding, that one is not fully satisfied until he purposefully gives himself to God.

Llull's conversion appears to be a common conversion experience as described by St. Paul in Romans 7:7–25. It is the two-ways paradigm of presenting a human's failure and the threat it poses (eschatologically), mainly death.[14] Llull spent sleepless nights concerning this troubling vision and the challenge it posed. He prayed and meditated on what this all meant personally and how it would change the trajectory of his life. Anthony Bonner writes concerning what Llull concluded of this matter:

> At last as a gift of the Father of lights,[15] he thought about the gentleness, patience, and mercy which Christ showed and shows towards all sorts of sinners. And thus at last he understood with certainty that God wanted him, Ramon, to leave the world and dedicate himself totally to the service of Christ.[16]

Llull gave himself to Christ, all the while thinking to himself what kind of service could he render to one who had forgiven him of so much. The timeframe is unknown, but it is believed by many hagiographers that Llull made his mind up rather quickly that he would reach the Saracens for Christ. Muslims could be found in Spain, Europe, and of course North and West Africa, all in proximity to Catalonia. Llull also recognized he was underprepared to take on this task, so he was saddened by his unpreparedness. Years later, Llull would write about his conversion. Unlike Augustine of Hippo, who wrote about his past and repented of such a wayward life, confessing the greatness of God and his graciousness toward this young sinner, all the while confessing various sins and lamenting, Llull reflected how his conversations with God led him first to penitence and then to a new

---

13. Bonner, *Ramon LLull*, 31–33.
14. Blackwell, Goodrich, and Maston, *Reading Romans in Context*, 93–98.
15. A reference to Jas 1:17.
16. Bonner, *Doctor Illuminatus*, 12.

birth.[17] Almost immediately, Llull knew, through these conversations with God, that he needed three things: (1) a willingness to die in service of his Lord in reaching the Saracens, (2) to compose the greatest book that would counter the errors of all pagans; and (3) be a catalyst of the establishment of training centers and monasteries to learn the language of the Saracens.[18] It would be the second goal that involved most of his life. This should not have been unexpected since he spent most of his youth and young adult life writing sonnets and songs. Writing, for Llull, was a way to give back to God for having forgiven him of his great sinful life. It was also a way of communicating with the One who spoke to him, first in visions, then through conversations concerning his life and morals. It was Llull's manner of both speaking of God's love and responding to that same love.

After taking stock of how unprepared he was to accomplish these three tasks, a deep gloom overcame Llull. He focused on working on writing a book, written so well and against the heresies of unbelievers, that no one could refute its truth. However, once again, the task of doing this seemed impossible, for Llull saw the inadequacy of his own ability. Though firmly believing that God wanted him to set out to do these three tasks, Llull beseeched the Lord to allow him to do these things for his Glory. Llull went to a church near him and begged God, with tears of devotion, to bring about a way for him to achieve these tasks. It appears that Llull, after having prayed this prayer, still had too many worldly ideas swimming in his head and heart, and returned to a lukewarm existence for a period of three months.[19] October 4, 1266, on the Feast of St. Francis, Llull heard a sermon about the life and ministry of St. Francis of Assisi—how the great saint had traveled to spread the gospel and rejected all goods and possessions in order to lead an unencumbered life to better serve his Savior. Roused by this example, Llull sold his possessions and set out on pilgrimages.[20] The selling of his possessions has been criticized by modern writers and historians because, by having a family, such measures would obviously hurt those he left behind. Llull left money and secured property for the support for his wife and children. This practice, though not common, was not frowned or judged negatively by either the church or society. The details of his conversion and dedication are important because Llull is forming a spiritual reality that would guide him throughout his ministry. Concerning his conversion, Llull later wrote,

---

17. Vega, *Ramon LLull and the Secret of Life*, 3–4.
18. Vega, *Ramon LLull and the Secret of Life*, 4.
19. Bonner, *Doctor Illuminatus*, 12–14.
20. Barber, *Raymond Llull*, 20.

When I was grown and knew its vanities, I began to do evil and entered on sin. Forgetting the true God I went after carnal things. But it pleased Jesus Christ in His great pity to present himself to me five times as if crucified, that I might remember Him and set my love on Him, doing what I could that the truth be taught concerning the great Trinity and the Incarnation. And thus I was inspired and moved by so great love, that I loved no other thing but that He should be honoured, and I began to do Him willing service.[21]

Llull's conversion experience gave him a new perspective on life, both from a personal and a cosmological view. Not speaking of his past enabled him to move away from it into the newness that comes only through an actual transformation. He thought of earthly experience as temporal and fleeting. However, the cosmological perspective gave him a universal language of redemption and repentance that he could share with others. Llull's awakening gave him a new perspective on reality, how selfish love leads to death and how Christ now offers a life, a cure for the death of the old life, which is much more meaningful and true. He did not dwell on the carnal life but on God's purposefulness in forgetting the former life and its *concupiscentia carnis*, or the lustful longing of the flesh.[22] Llull strongly felt the call to dedicate his life to the propagation of the faith without retreating himself to a monastery. The fact that he desired to go back into the world immediately exhibits a character that breaks from the tendencies of his day to live a separate (from the world) life and engage the pagans with the gospel. He did renounce the world, but understood immediately the heart of God in attempting to reach the lost in the world.[23]

ASSISI, AUGUSTINE, AND ANSELM

One of the advantages, if it can be called thus, of Llull not furthering his education, as his parents wanted him to, was that he would not learn the methodology of a system and terminology of medieval education, that is, of repeating and memorizing commentaries by other authors and never thinking independently and innovatively. As a nonprofessional, he thought he was being innovative, but in reality, was repeating much of what was known concerning doctrines and methodologies. This explains why, to some extent, Llull ran into difficulties in communicating what he wished to express.

21. LLull, *Book of the Lover and the Beloved*, 3–4.
22. Vega, *Ramon LLull and the Secret of Life*, 5–6.
23. Ruiz Simon and Soler Llopart, "Ramon Llull in his Historical Context," 47–61.

Llull directed his expressions toward effectiveness rather than eloquence or correctness. He did not write his first major work until several years after conversion and had returned from a pilgrimage. He did study the writings of the Fathers on his own, yet authorized church leaders helped him along in his independent studies. Though the intellectual life was reserved for specialists who studied philosophy and church history, many laymen were allowed to study alongside these specialists. Llull studied theological trends of his day, yet remained a freethinker. It was not long after his initial studies that he believed he needed a period of seclusion to better organize his thoughts and approach to teaching the truths he learned. He secluded himself in Mont Randa near Palma in Majorca.[24] For Llull, writing the "best book" became an integral drive in his spiritual life early on and throughout his life. Full of this drive, he left for the University of Paris to study grammar and dialectic science. His skill at writing and mental vigor was an advantage in his studies. Hence, the reason he so speedily conceived of the apologetic literature for his future missionary activity.

Medieval spirituality in the Spanish peninsula often used trees, birds, and plants, or other forms of nature as analogies of the church or Christian life. Llull also used such analogies in his writings, which is not to say these analogies have not been utilized throughout the history of the church, for even Jesus of Nazareth used examples from nature to teach spiritual truths; however, in the Iberian Peninsula, these were highly utilized in devotional life and studies on the Christian life. Both Castilian and Catalonian literature avoided the imagery of a crucified Christ and instead chose to substitute the image of a battered Christ with forms from nature. These nature motifs appear from the thirteenth century to the early fifteenth century.[25] Church teachers and polemicists did not consider it fruitful to use the images of Christ's torture and death for the purposes of conversion. Perhaps Muslim influence on the denial of the entire passion narrative had influenced the Iberian Christians to not focus on the crucifixion, or the Messiah hanging on a cross of wood, or any particular aspect of this death. In addition, many Jews still lived in the peninsula and perhaps it was out of respect for the Jewish population to not emphasize the passion imagery. Llull's conversion of the crucified Christ obviously challenged this tendency, for he had seen the crucified Lord calling out to him, until he finally submitted his life. After arriving at Mont Randa, Llull continued to have these visions of the cross, of Christ hanging on the tree. Llull saw the risen Lord, still displaying the scars of suffering and torture. For Llull, these visions came in the

24. Ballard, "Ramon Llull–Doctor Illuminatus 1235–1315," 212–14.
25. Robinson, "Trees of Love, Trees of Knowledge," 392–93.

same intensity as the first visions; wondrous trances that revealed to him the spiritual rapture of realizations of both the sorrows and awareness of a resurrected Christ.[26] Llull wrote two works using the tree metaphor in the titles: *Arbre de Ciencia* (*Tree of Knowledge*) and *Arbre de Filosofia d'Amor* (*Tree of the Philosophy of Love*).

Looking further at Llull's spirituality, it is understood no spiritual tradition arises in a vacuum. A couple of hundred years before, Anselm had written about the sufferings of Christ and how Christians should contemplate the sufferings of Christ to fully understand his love and heroic sacrifice for humanity.[27] This motif was prevalent in Christianity throughout Western Europe. It had even reached the Iberian Peninsula, but through the next two centuries this theme was suppressed by Muslim rule in Spain. Even Christians minimized its importance. The emphasis in Spain changed to how the debtor should remember the great cost of his salvation and elevated Jesus Christ to a heroic stature, and to the importance of bearing fruit and seeking further revelation of God.[28] Tree imagery was utilized by Llull to explain the incarnation. He believed this explanation would convert sinners to God, even though he had seen visions of the crucified Christ prior to his conversion. He wrote of trees as tools to meditate on the characteristics and attributes of God. There was a deep concern for the inward life in his writings and he felt the best way to teach about the inner life was through natural imagery. In fact, late medieval spirituality focused on the inward life of the believer. This was not the only time in church history that the inner life was the focus, but given the uncertainty of the times, the concern for the inner life gripped many, whether clergy or laity. Llull acquired this discipline from spiritual fathers of his day and perpetuated the same practice in his writings. Llull fully believed in Anselm's dictum from the *Proslogium* that stated, "He is better who is good to the righteous and the wicked than he who is good to the righteous alone."[29] Llull was not denying that God was just but emphasizing that God was a merciful God who showed a great sinner such mercy and kindness as himself. Here, Llull was influenced by Anselm's warnings against Christians seeking vengeance. Llull became an adherent to the imitation of Christ as a call to build up the inner life in his daily journey with Christ.

Catholic Mendicant orders like the Franciscans helped promote the mystical life. These orders also promoted an industrious attitude toward

26. Barber, *Raymond Llull*, 23–24.
27. Heckman, "Imitatio in Early Medieval Spirituality" 144–47.
28. Robinson, "Trees of Love, Trees of Knowledge," 397–99.
29. Deane, *St. Anselm, Basic Writings*, 14.

missionary activity. For Llull, this translated into an intense prayer and inner life dedicated to transformation and renewal as well as developing a heart for the lost. The writings of St. Bonaventure of Bagnorea in Tuscany, a Franciscan monk, were an influence in Iberian spirituality at this time. Bonaventure attempted to integrate reason and faith through the combination of Anselm's idea of a being which "nothing greater can be conceived" and with Neoplatonic metaphysics of Aquinas.[30] Bonaventure was a meditative scholar who wrote many devotionals and influenced the Franciscan order in this application. Llull read and understood the teachings of Bonaventure, his contemporary, in such a way as to imitate this great thinker. In his book *The Journey of the Mind into God*, Bonaventure wrote that Christ, being the perfection of God, was the greatest theological truth from three aspects: the symbolic, the literal, and the mystical. In the symbolic and mystical, perception and emotion explained these truths, but in the literal, the mind was of great importance to rationalize what the symbolic and the mystical meant.[31] Llull approached the faith in such a way as to see beyond the earthly physical world and understand that believers must sense or perceive the invisible yet eternal world before anything else. As for the mystical, Llull wished that the world should be won over through "love and prayers" rather than through might and sword. Llull's conviction of love's superiority over might was the driving force to which he was dedicated, coupled with the desire to please his Lord.

Some have criticized Llull's efforts to reach out to Muslims of his day using logic and reason. However, this is a misunderstanding of what Llull was trying to accomplish. During this age it appears brute force was the only way to deal with the Muslim population of Southern Europe. Llull dreamt of a day when peaceful discussions and undeniable proofs of God's goodness and grace would prove victorious over any false doctrine.[32] His steadfast belief in the superiority of the Christian doctrine over any pagan doctrine motivated him to pursue evangelism to Muslims and Jews. Llull believed it was ignorant to trust in might to force belief. He believed that the great strength of Christianity was its ability to convince one of the great moral truths. He also strongly felt that this knowledge must be mixed with belief. He often quoted St. Augustine's dictum of *Nisi credideritis, non intelligetis* or "unless you believe you will not understand." He differed from Aquinas' belief that natural reason would lead a person to faith in Christ. He believed the Christian faith was a logical and sublime faith, but nonetheless, the real

---

30. Saint Bonaventure, *Journey of the Mind of God*, 2–3.
31. Saint Bonaventure, *Journey of the Mind of God*, 7–8.
32. Barber, *Raymond Llull*, 26–27.

strength in Christianity stood from the truths. The unbelieving world would have to assimilate that which appeared illogical or unreasonable, such as the Trinity, the resurrection, or the incarnation. There is a story told of Llull encountering an educated Muslim ruler who challenged him to "prove to him that his faith (Llull's) was reasonable" and the ruler would convert immediately. Llull responded that Christian faith is "too sublime a thing to be proved." Llull used this story to warn missionaries to not get into such discussions, as it was useless to discuss Christianity only in philosophical terms.[33] Both Aquinas and Llull were missionary thinkers, but their approaches were polar opposites. Aquinas believed that philosophy may have been subject to error, theologically, but as a discipline, it could explain much of life's questions. Aquinas thought that philosophy could offer divine wisdom and therefore was a worthy discipline.

Llull belonged more along the lines of Assisi in terms of his spiritual practice. He identified more with the "ecstatic" type of Christianity that so dominated that period. The visions of Christ on the cross, the demonstrative response to follow Christ, and the emotional prayer life that would not stop until it had received revelation, or at least a peace overcame him, all played into his apologetic method. His intention was not to bring an intellectual knowledge to the Muslims but bring Christ to them and to the world.[34] Whereas Aquinas often left out preaching of the gospel (although he was very aware of the need for teaching), Llull's apologetic method frequently intermingled preaching and teaching. Llull believed these two disciplines were integral parts of bringing Christ to the world. He did not reject Aquinas teaching on the importance of philosophy, he just did not agree that philosophy alone was capable of bringing the lost to a complete and saving knowledge of Christ. Llull's philosophy mirrored that of Anselm's in that he employed more mysticism in his arguments than pure logic, and he would agree that faith precedes reason. He also wrote in meditative forms, ecstatic writings that expressed great love and admiration for his Lord.

Llull was convinced of his beliefs and his method for evangelism. He prepared for the mission field with great assurance of purpose and approach. While his country was engaged in a religious war and having great success at wiping out the enemy, Llull went about with great confidence that a peaceful, more spiritual approach could win the Muslims for the kingdom of God. St. Francis began this peaceful war when he reached out first to the Muslim world in love and compassion. In an era and area that saw atrocities committed in the name of religion, and witnessed the overthrow of Muslim

33. Schmidt, "Thomas Aquinas and Raymundus Lullus," 122–23.
34. Schmidt, "Thomas Aquinas and Raymundus Lullus," 135–36.

rule from the Spanish peninsula, Francis was the greatest example of love winning over violence. Francis' spirituality influenced many, most especially Llull, who were searching for more than just an existence. Francis' zeal to reach the Muslim world seems to have found a companion in Llull. Francis' bravery in reaching the Sultan and averting a war with Christian forces was no small matter in Llull's point of view. Francis' desire to be a martyr by putting himself in harm's way in going to the Sultan impressed Llull so much so that he sought to mimic Francis' life.[35]

Llull's early life of philandering proved to be his downfall, yet it was this miserable existence that led him to the great visions of the cross. He needed a new birth, since neither marriage nor fatherhood could reform or change his behavior. As a former troubadour, Llull was skilled at writing songs and sonnets and this skill benefitted him greatly in the service for his Lord. Llull gave up everything, including family, to serve God completely as a Dominican at first, and then later, felt more at home with the Franciscan order. Llull set out to write the "greatest book ever." A work that would teach the believer about the truth of the faith and would convert the unbeliever. He wrote mostly mystical works, perhaps much of these inspired by his active and long prayer life. It is said that his prayers would take him deep into the night until he was fixed on the "greatness of God and man's inconsistencies."[36] Llull's life was to become a life of prolific literary production. Even with his preaching and teaching schedule, he would write some two hundred and eighty works, some quite lengthy treatises. He wrote in Latin, French, Catalan, and Spanish.[37]

His conversion story sets the tone for the remainder of his experience as a believer. While composing a sonnet, one of questionable morals, Llull saw a vision of Christ on the cross suspended in mid-air. Then again, days later, he saw the Lord appear to him as in the previous visit. None of the first two visions changed his behavior until this same vision appears again a few days afterwards. It was on either the fourth or fifth visitation of Christ on a cross that Llull, wholly terrified of these visions, tried to apprehend the significance of the visions. He concluded that these visions were pointing him to give his life to Jesus Christ. After some resistance, there came a blend of overwhelming guilt and understanding that one is not fully satisfied until he purposefully gives himself to God. It was then that Llull gave his life to Jesus Christ. Llull understood that his conversations with God had led him to repentance and penitence and then to a new birth.

---

35. Barber, *Raymond Llull*, 22.
36. LLull, *Book of the Lover and the Beloved*, 11–13.
37. Lohr, "New Logic of Ramon Llull," 24–25.

Llull's spiritual progress did not really occur until that fateful day in 1266, on the Feast of St. Francis, where Llull committed himself fully to serving God. Sometime within a few days of the feast, he proposed that he needed to accomplish three things for the Lord: a willingness to be a martyr in the service of his Lord, to compose the greatest book that would counter the errors of all pagans, and establish training centers and monasteries to learn Arabic. His former life as a troubadour served him well now that he was using his gifts for service to God. In addition, his past service as a soldier was good training as he traveled and suffered doing mission work. His service as a page in the royal court of Majorca also came in handy in entreating popes and bishops for the establishment of training centers for future missionaries to Arabic people. His admiration of St. Francis played into the totality of his life. He not only mimicked the great saint in terms of continuing a dialogue with Muslims of his day, but he achieved a life-long quest of training others to do evangelism to Arabic Muslims in distant lands.

3

THEOLOGY AND PHILOSOPHY OF MINISTRY

HAVING BEEN RECOGNIZED AS a mystic, Llull's influence in missions was not appreciated during his time. Ramon de Peñafort and St. Francis of Assisi were recognized as pioneers, but it was not until after his death that Ramon Llull was understood as a great influence in the field of missions. Francis' work was mentioned in a previous chapter, and Ramon de Peñafort, as head of the Dominican Order around 1238, was responsible for encouraging the formation of training centers for missionaries (monasteries) that taught Arabic languages and the study of the Torah, Talmud, Koran, and the Hadith. However, the first training center set up appears to have been established in 1232, at Palma of Majorca, Llull's hometown and residence.[1] This training center was one of many set up in the Iberian Peninsula to refute and show the errors of non-Christian texts concerning God, salvation, and holy living. Unfortunately much of the apologetic of the Dominicans rested on showing the errors of the texts of their opponents, which led to endless debates and discussions that never resolved anything.

TRAINING CENTERS FOR EVANGELISM IN ARABIC

Living in Majorca, Llull learned enough Latin and Arabic to be able to express his thoughts and beliefs in these languages. He learned Arabic from a Muslim slave who was unaware of Llull's intent of evangelizing Muslim

---

1. Simón, "El Joc de Ramon Llull i la Significació de l'Art General," 47–48.

peoples. Given the large population of Muslims in and around Spain, Llull's desire to reach this great company could be understood as a grand endeavor in missionary work. Learning Arabic for missionary work was only one reason for acquiring this ability. He also sought to dispute with the Saracens concerning their theology and philosophy. Llull was skilled enough to accomplish these tasks and some speculate that it took him a year and a half to two years to learn Arabic well enough to do these things.[2]

The acquiring of a Muslim slave was an interesting side story of Llull's life. Llull acquired the slave for the sole purpose of learning the Arabic language. Perhaps the slave discovered the purpose of Llull's intentions, or it was just his Muslim religion and hatred of Christianity that caused him to curse Christ and the church. Llull learned that the slave had blasphemed the name of the Lord and was so incensed by this that he struck the slave several times. Again, it is speculation as to why the slave acted out, maybe it was after learning of Llull's intent to do apologetics to the Muslim world, but it was obvious he had a hatred for the Christian God. Filled a zeal for the faith, Llull struck the slave. Still stinging from this discipline, the slave began to plot against his master. On a certain day, he took a sword and attacked Llull. Llull managed to subdue the slave but did receive a serious wound. The slave was incarcerated while Llull recovered. During his convalescence, Llull pondered what he should do to the slave. If he forgave him, what about the sin of blasphemy and the danger the Muslim still posed. On the other hand, why not show the slave grace and exhibit the love of Christ to this lost Saracen. Llull prayed and agonized over the fate of the slave. Even while going to visit the slave once he had recovered from his wound, Llull still was unsure what to do. He was still wrestling with the decision, for part of him wanted to extend grace to this lost Muslim. Upon arriving at the place where the slave was detained, he learned that the slave had hanged himself. Perhaps he hanged himself out of despair or because death at the hands of infidels seemed blasphemous to him, but whatever the reason, Llull felt a sense of release that God had taken this decision from him and sealed the fate of the slave.[3]

Soon after this episode, Llull wished to learn at the University of Paris. Raymond de Peñafort, the high ranking Dominican, convinced Llull to stay in Palma and begin a training center for missionaries and for the teaching of the Arabic language. Peñafort was the man who brought the Inquisition to Spain and encouraged the teaching of Arabic and Hebrew for the conversion of Muslims and Jews. It was in La Palma that the first missionary school

2. Bonner, *Doctor Illuminatus: A Ramon LLull Reader*, 14–16.
3. Bonner, *Doctor Illuminatus: A Ramon LLull Reader*, 16–17.

began. In the thirteenth and fourteenth century the mendicant orders, the Franciscans and the Dominicans, were leading the way in teaching foreign languages for the purpose of preaching to the lost.[4] However, Arabic, Hebrew, and Syriac were the main focus of European evangelism and training. The hotbed of teaching Arabic was in Spain, due in large part to Llull's efforts. Among his peers, Llull was unique in his knowledge of the Arabic language. Upon returning from his pilgrimages after committing to serve God in a more profound way, he began to set up language training centers. Llull was very familiar with Arabic culture since Majorca was at one time under Muslim rule. He began the first school in his native Palma in 1276. He began with thirteen pupils at the College of the Holy Trinity for missionary work among the Muslims.[5] The school probably followed the same practices of other Dominican and Franciscan schools, teaching not only languages but philosophy and apologetic theology as well.

Little is known about the other language schools other than from Llull's writings. He wrote a brief tract in 1290, titled *Tractatus de modo convertendi infidels* or the "Inquiry Concerning the Method of Converting the Infidels." In his lifetime, Llull implored the favor of Popes Innocent III and Boniface VIII. Both mendicant orders, the Franciscans and the Dominicans, were focused on good homiletics as they stressed the importance of communicating the Word of God. The object was to inform and inspire. Scholasticism added a new dimension in the training of leaders from the standpoint that preachers and evangelists were informed concerning the Scriptures and philosophy. Therefore, preaching in Llull's day had a two-fold purpose: theology and pedagogy. Anselm's famous phrase, *fides quarens intellectum*, was the popular motto of the training instructors. The training center leadership held that faith comes before understanding, and only through faith could one understand the great truths of the faith. Though it looked like philosophy may have had a prominent role in the work of missions and evangelism, faith was not minimized as it continued to have a conspicuous role in the saving work of the convert. These training centers were not just for training preachers, they were centers for the rationality of the Christian faith.[6] These centers also had another role or intention. Raymond de Peñafort had more in mind than just refuting Islam by encouraging Llull. These centers served as centers for the expansion of religious, political, and cultural realities of Aragon and Catalan Christianity. The main manual for these training centers was Thomas Aquinas' work *Summa contra Gentiles*. Aquinas' assertion

---

4. McCarthy, "Ramon Llull and the Teaching of Foreign Languages," 2.
5. McCarthy, "Ramon Llull and the Teaching of Foreign Languages," 7.
6. Casanovas, *La Novela Ejemplar de Ramon Llull*, 30–35.

was that philosophy was a perfect and noble quest because man resembles God more so when pursuing wisdom.[7] Yet, this inquiry should lead to the divine being, otherwise this exercise is futile. Faith is never foolish; it is best when it is informed, so thought Aquinas. Besides this work and learning Arabic, and many of Llull's writings served as instruction books for the missionaries. Probably the *Ars Magna* and his *Abre de Sciencia* (his great Art and the "Tree of Knowledge") were among the first training texts used. Also used was his work *Blanquerna*, a didactic teaching in the Christian life whose aim was to promote missions to Muslims and the rest of the unbelieving world.[8] Other training centers started from 1276–92, in Montpellier, France, near the Catalan border, Toledo, and in Paris. There was even a training center in the Papal court in Rome. Llull exceled in creating a missionary method and vocabulary. He created a preaching idiom in Catalan that both expounded and taught the great truths of the faith (incarnation, Trinity, and resurrection).[9]

Oddly enough, Llull was not the first to learn and teach Arabic in Spain. The Spanish peninsula was quite the center for the study and teaching of the Arabic language before Llull took the mantle of leadership in this area. In the early part of the twelfth century in the former center of Muslim religious activity, Toledo, a man by the name of Dominic Gundisalvus began translating Arabic works of philosophy and science.[10] It was perhaps this activity that inspired the need to translate Arabic works for the purposes of missionary activity, first by Peñafort, then Llull. However, Llull's dream was far beyond any plan ever pursued by any scholar or evangelist. Llull entreated both the King of France, Philip the Fair, in 1293, and Pope Clement V. The actual meeting with King Philip was so that the king could entreat the Pope to recover the Holy Land for Christianity. Though he detested the crusades soon after his conversion, he later saw them as useful tools to recapture the Holy Land for the faith. The king of France also longed to recapture the Holy Land, although for political gain, so the coming together of the court along with Llull's vision made a perfect union for this venture. Llull imagined a great military effort from the Mediterranean coast and on to Syria, laying that kingdom waste, then on to Egypt. From there, he saw a rapid conversion to Christianity from the infidels of those lands by use of rational and irresistible apologetics. His knowledge of Arabic culture and

---

7. Aquinas, *Summa Contra Gentiles*, 61.
8. Casanovas, *La Novela Ejemplar*, 52–53.
9. Casanovas, *La Novela Ejemplar*, 77–78.
10. McCarthy, "Ramon Llull and the Teaching of Foreign Languages," 7–9.

language, as well as Muslim philosophy and theology, made him a valuable asset in this venture.

The Council of Vienne met in October of 1311, to consider matters of a crusade, as well as other church reforms. Even though the crusade never was realized, Llull addressed the council by presenting his proposals for a language missionary school, and even read some of his poetic works in order to inspire the council. The council must have been impressed because his proposals were instituted in canon eleven of the council's decrees. It read,

> Among the cares lying heavily upon us there is one on which we reflect constantly: how we may lead the erring into the way of truth and win them for God with the help of his grace.... We are in no doubt that to attain our desire, the word of God should be fittingly explained and preached to great advantage. Nor are we unaware that the word of God is learned in vain and returns empty to the speaker if it is directed to the ears of those ignorant of the speaker's language. We are therefore following the example of him whom we, though unworthy, represent on earth. He wished that his apostles, going through the whole world to evangelize, should have a knowledge of every tongue. We desire earnestly that holy church should be well supplied with catholic scholars acquainted with the languages most in use by unbelievers. These scholars should know how to train unbelievers in the Christian way of life, and to make them members of the Christian body through instruction in the faith and reception of sacred baptism.
>
> In order, then, that skill in these languages be attained by suitable instruction, we have stipulated, with the approval of the sacred council, that schools be established for the following languages wherever the Roman curia happens to reside and also at Paris, Oxford, Bologna and Salamanca: that is, we decree that in each of these places there should be catholic scholars with adequate knowledge of Hebrew, Arabic and Chaldaic [Syriac]. There are to be two experts for each language in each place. They shall direct the schools, make faithful translations of books from these languages into Latin, and teach others those languages with all earnestness, passing on a skillful use of the language, so that after such instruction these others may, God inspiring, produce the harvest hoped for, propagating the saving faith among the heathen peoples. The salaries and expenses of these lecturers in the Roman curia will be provided by the apostolic see, those at Paris by the king of France, and those at Oxford, Bologna and Salamanca by the prelates, monasteries, chapters, convents,

exempt and non-exempt colleges, and rectors of churches of England, Scotland, Ireland and Wales, of Italy, and of Spain respectively. The burden of contributing shall be imposed on each in accordance with the needs of the faculties, notwithstanding any contrary privileges and exemptions, which however we do not wish to be impaired in other respects.[11]

The council's reaction to Llull's address must have seemed like a victory for Llull, considering the response came in formal language from the council. Unfortunately there was no mention of any steps needed to implement the plan for training centers. Canon eleven appears to have had little to no practical impact. Though the decree failed to act on its decision, it was regarded as valid by another church council. The Council of Basle in 1434, took up the subject and renewed the decree of 1311. However, this action was also ineffective as the original decree since it did not follow through with any practical steps of implementation. Many historians believe that the challenges of international politics was the downfall (or neglect) of many of Llull's ventures into establishing training centers. It certainly was not Llull's fault as he was extremely industrious and eager to present his case to any monarch and pope that would listen. Being Catalonian probably did not help his cause either, in fact, it may have hurt his chances of success. He encountered resistance from both Spanish and French kingdoms. The monarchs of these kingdoms were not entirely convinced that outreach to Muslims was necessary, and certainly not a priority. Both kingdoms had pretty much decimated the Muslim communities in Europe.[12] Llull's persistence was admirable and dauntless. Even though the king of France and some popes were willing to hear him out, they remained largely uninterested. Llull's persistence managed to impress the great Franciscan, Arnaldus de Villa Nova, who considered Llull a "great modern messenger of truth."[13]

LOVE FOR GOD HOLDS HIM CAPTIVE: THE REAL REASON FOR HIS DRIVE

Llull longed for the crown of martyrdom. Like many of those in the Franciscan order, he strongly desired to die as a martyr, for the cause of the One who gave his life for many. In a sense, it was their own spiritual crusade to die serving their Lord. In this age, Bernard of Clairvaux wrote to the

---

11. McCarthy, "Ramon Llull and the Teaching of Foreign Languages," 379–80.
12. Hillgarth, *Ramon Lllull and Llullism in Fourteenth Century France*, 28–29.
13. Hillgarth, *Ramon Lllull and Llullism in Fourteenth Century France*, 52–55.

Templars, "The soldier of Christ is safe when he slays, safer when he dies. When he slays, it profits Christ; when he dies it profits himself."[14] It is possible to draw a parallel between St. Paul and Llull in regard to their spirituality, visions, hard work, passions, and sufferings. Both were consummate workers for the Lord Jesus Christ. Their missionary zeal coupled with a rational explanation and defense of the faith, as well as their love for the lost (St. Paul for the pagans and Jews, and Llull for the Muslims) made the comparison interesting. Llull saw Christ's virtues as the greatest apologetic against any Muslim theology. The combinations of virtues could certainly prove both the Trinity and the incarnation.[15] The thirteenth and fourteenth centuries saw a tremendous increase in the concern for the "inner life" both from laity and clergy. Llull, like many others, was swept up in this wave of spirituality. In fact the inner life was so emphasized that there was little concern for the outer life, and many neglected and even abused their bodies and physical welfare because of this new focus. There was a growing interest to private prayer, and a renewed interest in Scripture reading.[16] This medieval spirituality eventually influenced much of the thought and practice of the Reformation. With such an emphasis, Llull never lost track that education was also a key component of one's spirituality. Llull displayed his spirituality early on through poetry, lest one forget he was once a troubadour.

In *The Art of Contemplation*, Llull wrote in mystical tones, yet never omitted the didactic element. It is written in intellectual language, but has a tender speech that focuses on the divine essence. It had been said that no tradition (spiritual) arises in a vacuum, so one also can say that Llull was influenced by Anselm's writings and St. Francis' missionary zeal. Llullist enthusiast and translator, E. Allison Peers, states that Llull wrote "full of the purest and noblest spirituality, compounded with the quintessence of love."[17] His inspirational writings can be summed up in the phrase Llull coined, "He who loves not lives not." Though unlike many of his contemporaries, Llull did not live the cloistered life, nor did he aspire to. He was engaged in the world, thinking of how to please his Lord while also seeking to bring the lost into the kingdom.

His life was full of excitement and adventure, filled with travels, danger, and political intrigue. In all this, his zeal was evident, even though he went through a personal crisis later in life that caused him great doubt, and

---

14. Zwemer, *Ramon LLull: First Missionary to Moslems*, 66–67.

15. Glymour, et al., "Ramon Llull and the infidels.," 136.

16. Kieckhefer, "Land of Lost Discontent: Classics of Late Medieval Spirituality, 82–85.

17. LLull, *Book of the Lover and the Beloved*, 2.

even depression. Besides *The Art of Contemplation* (*Ars de Contemplacio*), two other classics display his spirituality at its keenest: *The Book of the Lover and the Beloved* (*Libre de Amich e Amat*) and *Blanquerna*, both written in the Catalan tongue. Many researchers of his life have concluded that *Blanquerna* may have been an autobiography set in a fictional story. Llull uses the main character, Blanquerna, to display segments of his life. If this is so, then one can confidently state that Llull had a full and working prayer life. This prayer life is displayed in his passage from the *Book of the Lover and the Beloved* describing the prayer life of the main character: "Being then in his hermitage he would rise at midnight, and, opening the windows of his cell, would fall to contemplating the heavens and the stars, and praying with all possible devotion, that his soul might be fixed on God alone."[18] It is believed that this behavior was in Llull's faith and practice. *The Book of the Lover and the Beloved* goes on further to state,

> After sunset, he went up to the terrace, and there remained long in devout meditation, his eyes fixed on the heavens and the stars, discoursing with himself on the greatness of God and man's inconsistencies. In this state he remained until he retired to rest, and such was the fervor of his contemplation that even upon his bed he found himself in mystic converse with the All-Powerful.[19]

This high mystical expression and life was accompanied with a great regard for Scripture and his relationship to the Lord. Llull spent many days in some sort of sacred retreat being refreshed and inspired from both God and nature. In *Blanquerna*, Llull describes the ideal religious life lived by Blanquerna. Blanquerna's parents want to entrust him with their estate, but Blanquerna admits that he wants to live a life of a hermit (cloistered and separated for his Lord's work), so his parents arrange a marriage for him in order to dissuade him from being a hermit. Blanquerna convinces the girl to enter a convent, suggesting that the cloistered life is far better for the Christian, and she eventually becomes a nun. Blanquerna ultimately becomes the Pope and his would-be-fiancé becomes a nun and rises to abbess of a monastery. The entire story is an account of what Llull believed to be the highest ideal: a life lived in religious contemplation and service. *Blanquerna* ends with the pope, now very aged, renouncing his high office to spend his last days in seclusion in contemplation and prayer.

The Art of Contemplation is written in more transcendent language and is full of doctrinal teaching. It is centered on what Llull believed were

18. LLull, *Book of the Lover and the Beloved*, 12–13.
19. LLull, *Book of the Lover and the Beloved*, 13.

the three faculties of the soul: (1) the will, (2) the understanding, and (3) memory. These three faculties act as the main characters of this mystical novel.[20] This novel also acts as the fictitious work of Blanquerna, who attempts to show how the divine virtues should be contemplated through the three main characters. Many believe that this novel was an attempt to explain his "Great Art." Through these three faculties, he attempts to understand virtues such as eternity, power, wisdom, love virtue, truth, glory, perfection, justice, liberality, mercy, humility, dominion, and patience. The focus of Llull's spirituality was the Godhead, always contemplating the virtues and applying intellect with revelation of the Spirit as the main source of acquiring knowledge of the Holy. Llull was thoroughly convinced that if men could be shown the virtues of God in a rational manner, unbelieving men would surrender their lives to God. He also believed this would unite the three Abrahamic faiths into one faith under Christ. The Anglican journal *Modern Churchman* said it best when describing Llull's spirituality and missionary heart:

> In an age when the Church slaughtered heretics, offered to Jews and Moors the alternatives of baptism or exile, taught that Crusaders who fell fighting against Saracens passed straight to Paradise, Llull perceived that the wrath of man worketh not the righteousness of God, and resolved to convert Mohammedans to Christianity by Christian means.[21]

Llull's belief was that if the Holy Land was to be conquered, it would be by love, prayers, and sacrifice, and not by force.

The *Ars de Contemplacio* begins with enumeration and expounding the virtues of God. It is an ecstatic realization of how wonderful and sublime God's virtues are and speaks so profoundly of this deity that the author is moved emotionally in contemplating his greatness. Each virtue[22] is expounded and gloried, and God is given more glory for having them, so much so that Blanquerna is moved to humility, repentance, and a greater love for his Lord and Savior. However, the *Ars de Contemplacio* is not just a mystical work; it is used as a defense for important Christian doctrines. Blanquerna marvels at the unity of God acknowledging that God is one and complete, yet goes on to wonder at the Trinity and how essential all three persons of the Trinity are, not only in relation to one another but necessary

---

20. Llull, *Art of Contemplation*, 9–20.
21. Major, "Apostle of Algeria: Raymond Llull, 1236–1315," 330–32.
22. The virtues previously listed are eternity, power, wisdom, love virtue, truth, glory, perfection, justice, liberality, mercy, humility, dominion, and patience.

for the believer and the work on earth. Contemplating the Trinity, Llull writes,

> And therefore the perfect Justice, Wisdom, Love, Perfection, Glory, and Truth of God signified to Blanquerna that the world had had a beginning, and that the Work of the Divine Essence in Itself, whereby the Father begat the Son, and that the Holy Spirit proceeded from the Father and the Son, is a Work infinite, eternal and wholly perfect.[23]

This writing was a not so subtle attempt at apologetics as well as a work of spiritual formation for the believer. Llull also addressed the topic of the Incarnation in this work, stating, "It was fitting that God should take on human nature, in which and through which should be shown forth his Divine Persons."[24] Llull was conscious of the culture and the greatest need within it–to acknowledge the superiority of Christ and his church. In a land with a strong Christian, Jew, and Muslim presence, he was aware what issues needed to be brought forth in order to bring about spiritual awareness. Llull did not minimize any aspect of the Godhead in this work, devoting a chapter to the Father (Pater Noster). He acknowledges that the Father is higher than any creatures without diminishing the role and standing of the Son and the Holy Spirit. Then, He used Jesus' teaching on prayer to show that the Father was not minimized in Christian worship. In referencing the "Our Father," Llull states,

> By which heights and excellences Thou dost make known in the Pater Noster that Thou art Father, because Thou art higher than all creatures, and because in Thy heavens are Thy works, whereby Jesus Christ called Thee Father, of himself and of us. Wherefore if Jesus Christ, Who is God and Man, in the heavens and equal with Thee as touching His Godhead, and upon the earth as touching His Manhood, bears Thee Witness that Thou art His Father and ours and art in the Heavens, it is meet and right that we, who are here below on earth, should believe His witness and say this prayer of Pater Noster.[25]

Llull goes on to extol the beauty of the Ave Maria, praising Mary for her sacrifice and love of God. He includes chapters on the Commandments, the Seven Sacraments of the Holy Church, and a penitential prayer derived from Psalm 51, called the *Miserere Mei Deus* (Have Mercy on Me

23. Llull, *Art of Contemplation*, 52–53.
24. Llull, *Art of Contemplation*, 58.
25. Llull, *Art of Contemplation*, 67.

God), emphasizing the need for deliverance and forgiveness from God. It is through this small work, though it is part of a larger work, that Llull teaches his readers about the important things within the Christian life and defends the key doctrines of the faith.

In his larger work (*Blanquerna*), Llull's teachings are more general, but they cover a larger span of life. He addresses the virtues all Christians should pursue through a fictitious novel about a young couple, Evast and Aloma, who have a son and it is through this child that they dedicated to serve God by making him a well-educated, respectful, and well-groomed individual. In *Blanquerna*, Llull extols the virtues of matrimony, religion, priorities,[26] Apostolic Estate,[27] and the monastic life (usually translated as the hermit life). Both *Blanquerna* and *The Art of Contemplation* display Llull's spiritual progress and development from his conversion and subsequent re-dedication. There were other influences, as shown in previous chapters, such as the language of nature being a vehicle he often used to express his spiritual knowledge and defense of his faith. He wrote *Arbol de Filosofia* (*Philosophy Tree*) and *Arbol de Ciencia* (*Tree of Knowledge*) to express both defense of his great work, *Ars Generalis*, and to further explain why the Christian faith is rational and superior to any religion. His use of nature as symbols of virtue probably proceeds from a Sufi and Kabalistic influence of his time.

Muslim Sufi philosophers taught a metaphysical love; that is, they often spoke of love in terms of a physical love. Sufis were condemned and incarcerated by Muslims in the tenth and eleventh centuries for teaching this type of love. Llull was inspired by Sufi mysticism and wrote along the same lines. Llull penned his most popular work, *The Book of the Lover and the Beloved* on this premise, as well as many other poems.[28] There are many expressions of love in the book, as if two lovers were interacting with one another. In one section, the lover is sick with love, very much reminiscent of Song of Solomon 3:1–5. Chapters 21 and 22 of this work, which are only short paragraphs, read,

> 21 The Lover came to drink of the fountain which gives love to him who has none, and his griefs redoubled. And the Beloved

---

26. The priorities spoken of are the formation of ecclesiastical governance, assistance to the poor, personal humility, contrition and brokenness, application of mercy in the believer's life, the avoidance of worldliness, living in peace, about persecution, and other difficult questions that must be addressed.

27. Apostolic estate is a justification for the papacy; it is a reference to apostolic succession. It shows how the pope should be elected, what qualities the pope and papal candidates exhibit, how the Pope set the example for living, and other qualities to look for in Popes and bishops. Over all things is God, who should to be worshipped properly.

28. Games, *Ramon Llull y la Tradicion Arabe*, 36–37.

came to drink of the same fountain, that the love of one whose griefs were doubled might be doubled also. 22 The Lover fell sick and thought on the Beloved, who fed him on His merits, quenched his thirst with love, made him to rest in patience, clothed him with humility, and as medicine gave him truth.[29]

Llull took up the Sufi concept of love but was careful not to confuse the two types of love to which the Sufis often fell victim. Llull believed one love was much higher than the other and was careful to distinguish this in his writings. He wrote in *The Book of the Lover and the Beloved*, "Ah entendimiento voluntad! Ladrad y despertad a los grandes perros que duermen olvidandose de mi Amado!"[30] Which is translated, "Will and understanding, bark and awaken the great dogs that sleep forgetting my beloved!" The lover in all this is the human and the beloved is Christ. Ibn al Arabi[31] a Sufi mystic living in Spain, once wrote using similar language, stating, "One of these lovers of God said: I am one who loves and who I love." The similarity showst hat Llull was inspired by these writings. Sufi mysticism enjoyed a golden age in the ninth and early part of the tenth centuries in Spain alongside Sunni Muslims. The two sects of Islam would eventually collide over these writings as well as other issues. Sunni Muslims avoided the language of the Spanish troubadours where physical love was often the topic of songs and poems. Llull, being a former troubadour, seemed comfortable expressing his faith in these terms.[32]

There are countless examples in *Blanquerna*, *The Art of Contemplation*, and *Book of the Lover and the Beloved* that describe Llull's personal view and approach to God. He was saved by fear, seeing visions of a crucified Christ that brought him dread, but it was hearing of the great sacrifice of St. Francis of Assisi and how his love for Jesus Christ inspired a missionary zeal and love for the lost that changed Llull so dramatically and thrust him into a deeper service and commitment to Christ. It was out of love that motivated him to reach out to the lost, primarily the Muslim community in Southern Europe and North Africa. His writings exhibit an ecstatic love for God that in many cases is hard to comprehend who (or what) he is talking about. In most other cases, one can discern, by the context, who is the object of his

---

29. LLull, *Book of the Lover and the Beloved*, 27.
30. LLull, *Book of the Lover and the Beloved*, 27.
31. Ibn al Arabi was a mystic who drew on the writings of Sufis, an Islamic theologian and philosopher, he was born in Murcia (in southeast Spain) in 1164, and died in Damascus in 1240.
32. Games, *Ramon Llull*, 47.

adoration and praise. Nothing exhibits his love and devotion more than his statement in *The Art of Contemplation* as Blanquerna states,

> You are infinite greatness in eternity, You are the good from which all good springs; all good things great and small come from Your great good, and all living things come from Your eternity. Because You are goodness and greatness, I adore You, call upon You, and love You above all that I can understand and remember, I pray that the good You have given me will stay with me, so I will be able to praise and serve You.[33]

In *Blanquerna* is a picture of Llull's devotional practices as he discusses the hermit life and the morning ritual of Blanquerna's successor as pope. He writes,

> Rising early in the morning, Blanquerna celebrated the Mass of the Holy Spirit. Later, the pope once again directed (in song) the solemn Mass then preached on the good and wise ordinances that his predecessor, Blanquerna had made in the same Court all for the fervor and desire to serve God more earnestly and higher, by leaving the papacy all for doing penance in the mountains, determined to be in the company of the trees, birds, and the beasts for the rest of his life, all for contemplating the Sovereign Lord God of Glory.[34]

The reference to nature as an ideal that leads one to a closer walk with God is a value often repeated in Llull's works. He writes in *The Book of the Lover and the Beloved*,

> The Beloved chastened the His Lover's heart with rods of love, to make him love the tree whence He plucks the rods wherewith He chastens His lovers. And this is the tree on which He suffered grief, dishonor and death, that He might bring back to love of Him those lovers whom He had lost.[35]

A PANORAMIC VIEW OF PHILOSOPHY OF MINISTRY

As previously stated, Llull wrote with the erudition of Bonaventure and the passion and devotion of Francis of Assisi. Like Bonaventure, Llull combined the contemplative mind and the heart in understanding God and spiritual

---

33. Llull, *Romancing God*, 70.
34. Llull, *Blanquerna: Maestro de la Perfeccion Christiana*, 320.
35. LLull, *Book of the Lover and the Beloved*, 69.

matters, and like St. Francis, he renounced all of this world's benefits for a better union with Christ. It is very likely he imitated the Sufi practice of speaking of physical love between a man and a woman as a metaphor to explain the higher love of God for humanity. One other practice, less discussed, is Llull's similarities with various Kabbalistic writings. Just as Llull wrote and combined God's virtues using concentric circles and other geometrical figures, a certain Kabbalistic school of ecstatic writings, identified as Scholem and Yates, also used similar figures and combinations but for different reasons. Llull used them for proving the unity of the Godhead and other doctrines, and the Kabbalah used the combination of the names of divinity in order to achieve ecstatic experiences.[36] Many of his other poems and songs were similar to the three major works discussed here. They were a combination of Muslim, Christian, and secular components. Nonetheless, these were all very Franciscan in tone and mysticism. At times they were apologetic, but most of the time they were great expressions of love and devotion, which is exhibited in his short story, *Felix*, or officially known as *Libre de Maravelles*.[37] There was a primary message and a secondary message in this work. The primary message was stated in the prologue: "That God may be known, loved, and served." The secondary message was a social criticism; a cause for what was wrong with the world, beginning princes, prelates, and the wealthy.[38]

The mysticism of Ramon Llull was a practical mysticism, that is, it concerned itself not with philosophy, but with personal salvation, which was common in the thirteenth century. Llull's passions served his flesh at one time in his life and now they served Christ and the church. His love for God demanded that he show that love to his fellow man. It was through poetry and writing that he channeled this love to teach and reach out to both the lost and the saved. This same love led him to write his great work, *Ars Major*, specifically to reach Muslims and any who differed or made less of the Christian God.

---

36. Idel, "Ramon Llull and Ecstatic Kabbalah," 172.

37. Many of Llull's works were renamed after the protagonist of the story. Blanquerna has a much longer named but is popularly known only as Blanquerna.

38. Bonner, *Selected Works of Ramon Llull*, 651–59.

4

APOLOGETICS AND AVERROES

"In the age of scholasticism, where many trivial questions were seriously debated in the schools, and philosophy was anything but practical, Llull proposed to use the great weapon of his age, dialectics, in the service of the Gospel and conversion of the Saracens."[1] So writes Samuel Zwemer concerning the age of evangelism of Ramon Llull. This quote does not affirm that Llull was not a scholastic, but his primary concern was missions. His philosophy was inspired by the gospel, love for Christ, and love for souls. Many have dismissingly laughed off Llull's dialectic of circles and tables, but one has to admire the zeal and earnestness with which they were created and presented. Llull desired to show a rational Christianity that the lost could not refute. Llull entered into a dialogue, somewhat, by reading Arabian philosophers and pointing out their errors. Llull understood that the strength of the Islamic faith was its philosophy; hence the reason he desired to engage the false premises of Islam.

The three prominent Muslim philosophers of Llull's day were Avicenna, Al-Ghazel, and Averroes. Llull's aim was to destroy their philosophic foundations by exposing false premises through reason and rational thinking. Llull's philosophy of missions included the study of geography as well. He believed that knowledge of the world was essential for creating a "republic of believers" and "conversion of unbelievers."[2] Llull believed the missionary unacquainted with geography is "not only ignorant where he

---

1. Zwemer, *Ramon LLull: First Missionary to Moslems*, 33–34.
2. Zwemer, *Ramon LLull: First Missionary to Moslems*, 35.

walks, but where he leads."³ This is quite a benchmark for missions in this age, as it exhibits a real pioneering spirit. Llull believed that the end of any geographical endeavor was the beginning of the missionary endeavor. Llull hoped for another age of Pentecost, but this time in Arabic lands.

APOLOGETICS TOWARD MUSLIMS—CULTURE AND FOCUS ON THIS GROUP

Historians have different opinions concerning Llull's work toward Muslims. Some have called him a crusader, encouraging military invasion and the reconquering of the Holy Land. Others have a more noble opinion of him, noting his desire to win the Muslims through reason. This work has noted that Llull's desire was to win unbelievers by reason, though later in life, he did support and encourage a crusade to the Holy Land, hoping the Christian army would be victorious so that he could then reason with the Muslims in the conquered lands and win them for Christ. This attitude was evident by his interview in 1294, with Pope Boniface VIII, where Llull submitted his "Petitio Pro Recuperatione Terrae Sanctae Et Pro Conversione Infidelium."[4] If Llull believed that Christianity was a rational faith, he also believed it was important to present the Jew and the Muslim as irrational. In the twelfth and thirteenth centuries, Jews, Muslims, and Christians often contended with conflicting claims of reason and revelation, wrestling with the difficult interactions between Scripture and philosophy, science, and competing religious traditions.[5] The one philosopher that carried the Aristotelian banner in thirteenth century Spain was Averroes. He was one of the "natural philosophers" who believed his sole duty was to find an agreement between religion and philosophy.[6] Averroes (otherwise known by his Arabic name as Ibn Rushd) received a privileged education, with studies in jurisprudence, theology, medicine, mathematics, and philosophy.[7] One item Averroes seemed to define thoroughly was the matter on the existence of the human soul after death. His ontology of the soul attempted to unify both philosophical and theological belief.

---

3. Zwemer, *Ramon LLull: First Missionary to Moslems*, 35.
4. Sanaullah, "Andalusian Seers, Sufi-Cristiano and the Cultism," 50.
5. Tolan, "Saracen Philosophers Secretly Deride Islam," 184–86.
6. González-Calderón, "Los Filósofos Naturales del Siglo XIII" 123.
7. González-Calderón, "Los Filósofos Naturales del Siglo XIII," 125.

AVERROES AND THE SOUL

Averroes strongly believed in the existence of the soul after death and believed it must be affirmed by religious doctrine, though the exact nature of the soul remained a mystery.[8] Averroes believed that the only way truths should be taught was through demonstrations and in books, otherwise it was futile to teach religious truths. This belief set him at odds with theologians of his own religion because religious teachers understood that not everything can be taught through demonstration, but through persuasive arguments and proofs from Scripture.[9] Other issues divided Averroes from Muslim theologians, including his thoughts on the human intellect, otherwise defined as the human potential. Aristotle was inclined to think that the human intellect was of a different character or substance from other faculties of the soul, but he never defined just how different or exactly what this nature was. The vagueness of his definition created more issues than enlightenment, especially among the Muslim philosophers. According to Averroes, the human intellect ranged from a "disposition" or a human having a state whereby they are disposed to have the ability to think and reason. This was his explanation for the physical body in the body-soul distinction. On the soul side of the spectrum, the intellect being, was a separate entity from the body, yet an incorporeal and indestructible substance.[10]

In his work, *De Anima*, Aristotle expressed the idea that the powers of the intellect must be in the soul. Aristotle believed the soul was immaterial and separate from the material body, which included the intellect that must be "uncontaminated and unmixed with the body."[11] Averroes added that the "material intellect"—the intellect situated in the physical body—needed the existence of an immaterial intellect to truly operate since it was not possible for the intellect to operate in a material form. Averroes believed that even the imagination needed an immaterial existence to operate. Llull did not thoroughly disagree with either of these philosophers on the soul, but his departure from them stems from what can be truly known. Llull argued that sense perception cannot be an acceptable basis for science and therefore the speculations on the soul were just reasonable theories. Llull contended that God was still the best and greatest source of knowledge, and it is through revelation one really understands. Llull believed faith is necessary, even vital, for one to understand the God of the Christian faith.

---

8. Taylor, "Averroes on the Ontology of the Human Soul," 580.
9. Taylor, "Averroes on the Ontology of the Human Soul," 581.
10. Davidson, "Averroes and Narboni on the Material Intellect," 176–77.
11. Taylor, "Averroes on the Ontology of the Human Soul," 583.

Understanding alone will not help one understand the Trinity, for instance. This understanding was a slight toward the Islamic belief that rational understanding can help one understand who and what God is. The Trinity exceeds senses and imagination, even though reasoning can usually be correct.[12] Llull taught that understanding was given to all men, as he appealed to general revelation endowed by the Creator to his creation. Faith, on the other hand, which surpasses understanding, is given as a gift by God. Some truths even understanding alone would not be possible to grasp. It is only through faith that one can truly know. This faith was in stark opposition to the Muslim philosophers of his day. Criticism of Christian faith may come because some claim that one cannot prove the claims of faith, therefore, an appeal to philosophy must be made in order to ponder these truths.

Llull felt that only faith can help one understand the eternal and infinite mysteries. The Trinity is one of these truths and human reasoning is inadequate to understand this mystery.[13] According to Llull, this proved the need for God in understanding the mysteries and for complete understanding of things infinite and eternal. Man alone cannot find God and he must go through God by faith for complete understanding of the universe. Otherwise, an infidel could destroy the faith of another if reason alone were to be used. Llull believed this because Christian-Muslim debates often centered on reason alone and nothing was gained. However, when certain Saracens would challenge the Christian to prove through reason why Christianity was superior to Islam, the Christian would also have to admit that this insistence and utter dependence on reason is an irrational demand. Christians must insist that faith is necessary and only God gives that.[14] Llull believed that the Saracen, if he wanted to convert to Christianity, must be infused with faith. Llull constantly contrasted faith and understanding not because he thought they were pitted against each other, but because both were necessary; yet, faith was equally if not more important to lead the believer into eternal truths. He placed these under the titles "Faith says" and "Understanding says":

> Faith says: the moment the Saracen converts to Christianity, he would be infused with faith.
>
> Understanding says: this is not true because he (Saracen) wants to understand the Trinity with only reason and it is not assured that God will give him the faith necessary to believe.

12. LLull, *Disputa Entre La Fe I L'Enteniment*, 20–24.
13. LLull, *Disputa Entre La Fe I L'Enteniment*, 90–97.
14. LLull, *Disputa Entre La Fe I L'Enteniment*, 99–101.

Faith says: demonstrable knowledge is not sufficient for understanding God, one must come to God, understand and get to know Him and talk to Him, then, and this can be done.

Understanding says: it is true there is no greater cause than God, but God is known and understood through reason and understanding certain properties.

Faith Says: How can understanding know that the Holy Spirit, distinct from God the Father, know that the Spirit cannot produce a divine person (Jesus Christ), as omnipotent as itself and the Father?

Understanding says: Just like God, whose unity is immensely great, so is His Fatherhood is immensely great and must be singular (or a singularity).

Understanding says: Many Christians doubt faith, and often ask if it is true. They do not honor you as they should. Their belief is more fiction that turns reality into a falsehood. Intelligent men understand the need for rational thinking.

Faith says: the more I am scorned, whoever honors and exalts me God will honor and exalt them.

Understanding says: Goodness and wholesomeness is an eternal quality but God has given all men the natural inclination to be good; we were created in His image. A man can reason to be good and live a good life.

Faith says: understanding is incorrect. Only God can produce goodness and wholesomeness for they are eternal qualities. Even reason and understanding are God-given abilities so man produces nothing.[15]

Llull introduced his Art (*Ars Generalis*) believing it was given to him by divine will. Llull never spoke ill of Islam, but he did often criticize Muhammed (Mahomet), and used his Art to display God's attributes in order to refute Averroes philosophy concerning the Divine Characteristics. For instance, Averroes believed God can be known primarily by his law and inference, meaning, his creation (nature). In other words, general revelation plays a vital role in Islam in order to "know" God. Llull showed that God's revelation of himself through Scriptures and individual enlightenment was far superior to any general revelation, and his attributes or virtues told the human much more about God the personal being. Figure 2 displays these attributes and how they interrelate to each other.

The A circle refers to divinity and has sixteen virtues: Goodness, Greatness, Eternity, Power, Wisdom, Will (exercise thereof), Virtue, Truth,

---

15. LLull, *Disputa Entre La Fe I L'Enteniment*, 111–41.

Glory, Perfection, Justice, Generosity (Grace), Mercy, Humility, Dominion, Patience.[16] Any two combined attributes will prove a truth about the Godhead: for instance, God cannot sin; any combination can prove this; will + power, or power + justice; or virtue + truth, etc.[17] For Llull, this proved the superior revelation of Christian Scriptures over any Islamic reasoning.

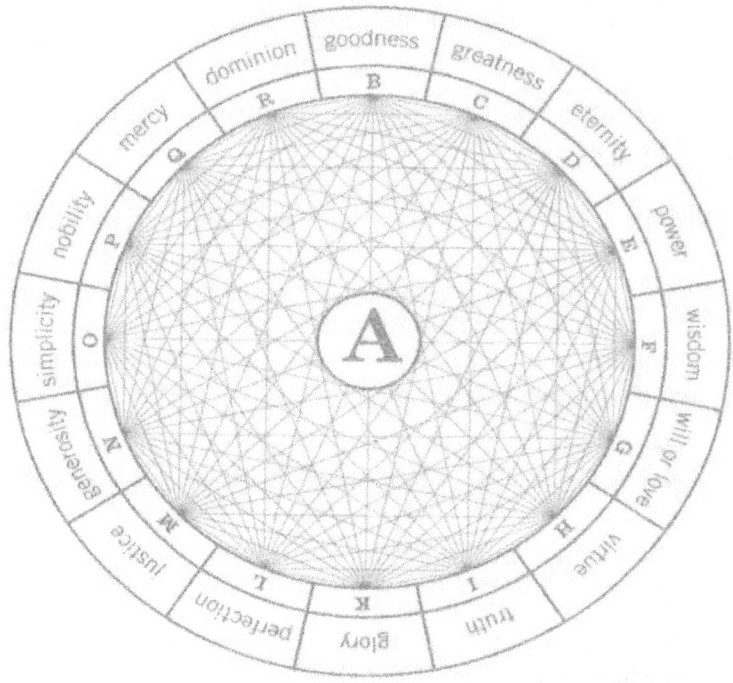

Figure 2. Attributes of God

Averroes wrote that philosophical reasoning was superior and believed reasoning from the Law or other revelation was futile. Specifically, Averroes wrote about the Islamic faith, "A large number of the followers of this religion confirm philosophical reasoning, all except a small worthless minority, who argue from religious ordinances."[18] He went on to add a justification for such reasoning:

---

16. Figure 2 is taken from Bonner, *Art and Logic of Ramon Llull: A User's Guide*, 93.
17. Llull, *Arte Breve*, 127.
18. Averroes, *Theology and Philosophy of Averroes*, 18.

> We Muslims should believe that rational investigation is not contrary to Law, for truth cannot contradict truth, but verifies it and bears testimony to it. And if that is so, and rational observation is directed to the knowledge of any existent objects, then the Law may be found to be silent about it or concerned with it.[19]

Averroes made the assumption that general revelation or at least human understanding was always in step with the divine Law. Llull made no such assumption as he believed divine Law and special revelation were distinct and superior to human reasoning from general revelation.

SPECIAL REVELATION AVAILABLE TO ALL

For all the claims and reliance on general revelation, Averroes often contradicted this claim by suggesting that not all humans could attain knowledge of the one true God. He referred to Avicenna's work *The Refutation of Philosophers*, stating that Islam recognizes that not all can reason and understand, therefore it is good to not teach the deeper things to those who are incapable of learning these truths:

> He [Avicenna] has explained that the infidelity of a man who ignores the consensus of opinion is doubtful. Moreover we have definitely pointed out that it is not possible to establish a consensus of opinion in such matters, especially when there are many people of the early times who have held that there are interpretations which should not be disclosed to all but only to those who are fit for them and those are men who are "well-grounded in knowledge" a divine injunction which cannot be overlooked. For if such people do not know the interpretation in these matters they will have no special criterion of truth for their faith, which common people have not, while God has described them as believing in Him. This kind of faith is always produced by the acceptance of the arguments, and that is not possible without a knowledge of interpretation. Otherwise, even the common people believe in the words of God without any philosophy whatever. The faith which the Quran has especially ascribed to the learned must be a faith strengthened with full arguments.[20]

Llull repeated that his Art had been given to him as an act of divine will in the form of a methodological and formal intuition of universal scope.

19. Averroes, *Theology and Philosophy of Averroes*, 26.
20. Averroes, *Theology and Philosophy of Averroes*, 33–34.

His wish to successfully communicate the Art to the most varied public made him see the need repeatedly to re-elaborate it, first in the direction of a growing enrichment, and later in that of a didactic stylization. He believed all could rationally come to the conclusion that the attributes of God could be communicated to all men through Scripture (special revelation) and through reasoning (general revelation). Though he stressed the importance of the need for God to reveal himself to the individual, he was convinced God wanted to do so. His attributes pointed to such a belief.[21] One can follow the line between mercy and truth in Figure 2, or from goodness and truth and deduct that God revealed himself to those who believed and to those who sought Him. Llull was referencing Isaiah 51:4–6 as God implores humanity to seek him since "all revelation flows from me." He may also have been referencing Isaiah 55 and/or Jeremiah 29:13 that encourages all to "seek God" because the assurance is "they will find Him." Figure 2 shows the attributes and the possible ways they can be combined, but these are only used to show how they can be combined and how these attributes can and do relate to one another. They are never used in the actual discourse of the art.[22] These attributes are essential virtues and are non-negotiable.

Llull uses another figure to illustrate virtues and vices (of mankind) as they relate to belief, and or lack thereof in God. It may illustrate how virtues relate to one another and how incompatible they are to the vices. Figure 3 illustrates this. The seven virtues are faith, hope, charity, justice, prudence, fortitude, temperance. The seven vices are gluttony, lust, avarice, pride, accidie (spiritual sloth, apathy, and/or indifference), envy, and ire. These virtues and vices stand in contrast to the perfect attributes of God. In figure 3, the vices connect to one another while the virtues only connect to other virtues.[23] This is a logical display as Llull believed vices and virtues cannot be present at the same time, as this would be illogical at least and hypocritical at worst. Llull followed the line that virtues are of one accord while vices of another.[24]

---

21. Llull, *Arte Breve*, 29.
22. Bonner, *Art and Logic of Ramon Llull*, 32.
23. Figure 3 is taken from Bonner, *Art and Logic of Ramon Llull*, 92.
24. Bonner, *Art and Logic of Ramon Llull*, 35.

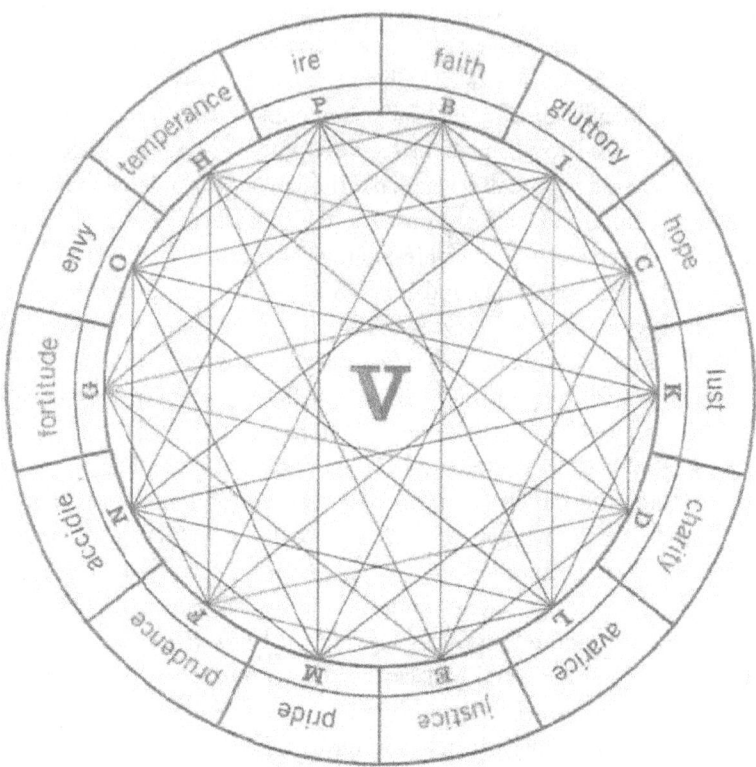

Figure 3. Virtues and vices

The central issue of these two figures is that figures 2 and 3 form the pillar of his "Art," including his other works such as *Blanquerna* (a tale of virtuous living), *The Book of Proverbs, Dispute between Faith and Reason, The Book of the Lover and the Beloved*, the *Art of Contemplation*, and his more concise, *Ars Brevis* (brief version of the Art).[25] Llull's method in creating these figures was to exhibit his *modus operandi*, which was to demonstrate truth. The demonstration of truth negates any falsehood and, as Bonner explains, Llull directed this Art primarily at Muslim philosophers to show that everything God created and made "He created and made in the likeness of his dignities."[26] Llull's work may have appeared idealistic and perhaps even unrealistic. No one really thinks in these terms, but he believed his Art exemplified and described true reality because the universe was created

25. Bonner, *Art and Logic of Ramon Llull*, 36.
26. Bonner, *Doctor Illuminatus: A Ramon LLull Reader*, 51.

with logic, which showed these true patterns of logic of the universe.[27] This work was not a body of doctrine but a system that displayed a totally structured universe. He insisted the purpose of the Art was to "understand and love God."[28] Its teaching are twofold: to convert the pagan and to instruct the believer. It gave unbelievers a perplexing argument to grapple with and confound their erroneous thinking concerning God and spiritual matters. The second figure was telling of his intent for the first figure. These virtues and vices could be used as a means at arriving at a knowledge of God. The idea for the believer and the seeker of truth was to learn to love virtues and hate vices. The second figure instructed the human in the right way to live in order to glorify his God and dispel doubt in one's life. In other words, Llull's belief was that the knowledge of virtues and vices and application of the former in one's life increased faith.[29] Llull also believed these virtues as well as Figure 2 helped "acquire other sciences," at least initially, and helped in the exploration and study of other sciences since these qualities and virtues created a good starting point in the investigation of all truth. These virtues were a form of revelation more specific than just human reasoning.

THE GODHEAD AS FOCUS OF REVELATION

Llull believed his *Art Magna* answered the skeptics concerning the Trinity. He responded to the false unitarian belief that only a single being (person) can be good. Using the Muslim philosopher's own words, he argued,

> Every being which is perfectly good is so perfect in itself that it does not need to do good, nor ask for any, outside of itself. You say that God is perfectly good from eternity and for all eternity, therefore He does not need to ask for, nor to do good outside himself; for if He did, He would then not be perfectly and absolutely good. Now since you deny the most blessed Trinity, let us suppose that it did not exist; in that case God would not have been perfectly good from eternity until He produced, in time, the good of the world. You do believe in the creation of the world, and therefore, when God created the world in time He was more perfect in goodness than before, since goodness is better diffusing itself than remaining idle. This, I claim, is your position. Mine however is that goodness is diffusive from eternity and for all eternity. And it is of the nature of the good that

---

27. Bonner, *Doctor Illuminatus: A Ramon LLull Reader*, 51.
28. Bonner, *Doctor Illuminatus: A Ramon LLull Reader*, 54.
29. Bonner, *Doctor Illuminatus: A Ramon LLull Reader*, 54.

it be diffusive in and of itself, for God, the good Father, from His own goodness generates the good Son, and from both is breathed forth the good Holy Ghost.[30]

It was comments such as these that often got Llull in trouble or nearly killed. He strongly felt the logic of the Art refuted any anti-Trinitarian belief. The Art, Llull believed, could be understood by any believer, whether an erudite or unlearned, and could know God and recognize his attributes. Llull believed these attributes helped form proper opinions about the Godhead. He was confident all believers could comprehend the significance of the attributes and apply the logic to their lives. Averroes displayed a skepticism concerning the abilities of some humans to understand from logic. He writes concerning certain Muslims who read and misunderstand philosophic works:

> For the majority cannot understand philosophic books, only those endowed with superior natures. People are on the whole destitute of learning and are aimless in their reading which they do without a teacher. Nevertheless they succeed in leading others away from religion.[31]

In *Blanquerna*, the main character looks upon the virtues of God claims that God has revealed these virtues to humankind. He recalls this power has all knowledge to go along with his great strength. He states, "You, O Knowledge, know even as You will. You, O Will, do will even as you will in will, power, and knowledge."[32]

APOLOGETICS–ANOTHER 'ART'

Ramon Llull's major work was not met with a lot of enthusiasm or interest. Perhaps it was too intricate and detailed for even the most educated of men. Perhaps it seemed impractical to those to whom he presented it. He was constantly trying to communicate this Art to his students, other clergy, and monarchs. Yet it was not accepted wholly nor was it readily understood. He truly believed and repeated that this Art was given to him as an act of divine will. The constant wish to successfully communicate the Art to the most varied public made him see the need repeatedly to re-elaborate it.[33] He later came up with a shorter, more concise version of his original Art,

30. Bonner, *Doctor Illuminatus: A Ramon LLull Reader*, 36–37.
31. Averroes, *Theology and Philosophy of Averroes*, 55–56.
32. Llull, *Romancing God*, 71.
33. LLull, *Arte Breve*, 127.

and naming it the *Ars Breve*. He still used the 'A' chart (figure 2), but also used other figures he used in the *Ars Magna*. For instance, he referred to chart 'S' where the letter 'S' refers to the rational soul of figure 4, as a more systematic way of presenting the concepts he addressed in his first Art. The first phase of the Art (1274–89), *Ars Compendiosa Inveniendi Veritatem*, established the figures and alphabets of Ramon's method for the first time: it was the central work of the first cycle of this phase. In the second cycle, Llull re-elaborated his system around the *Ars Demonstrativa* (1283).

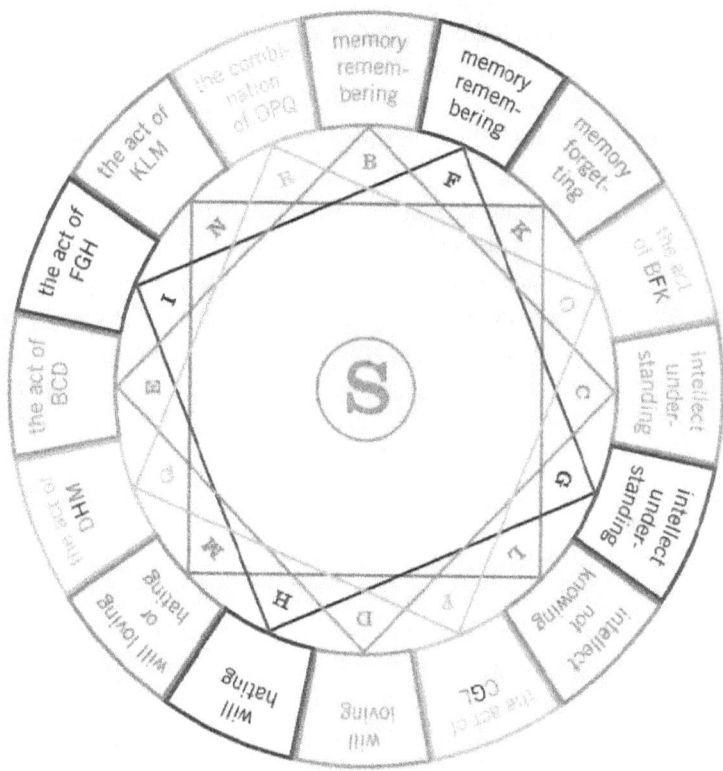

Figure 4. Powers of the soul

THE SOUL AS A MODEL OF THE TRINITY

Figure 4 is the most unusual figure in his Art.[34] It is based on Augustine's three powers of the rational soul: memory, intellect, and will.[35] The soul is not a collection of these three powers, but of their acts and combinations of acts. This figure is a vibrant exhibit of the actions and combinations of acts of an individual. The figure is not very helpful without an explanation and can be confusing. Llull fashioned it after a model for the Trinity. There are sixteen compartments, but not necessarily sixteen acts of the soul. Llull categorized this chart in this manner to visually show how these actions interact and develop. Llull usually referred to the square represented by the distinct color as one letter to indicate total actions combined. For instance, the action in blue is the act of remembering, understanding, and loving, or B, C, D. However, Llull would simplify this activity as E, or B+C+D=E. He did this for the other three combinations of activities as well, displayed by the distinct colors in the figure 4. This part of the Art, like the rest of the Art, was made for the purpose of persuasion on matters of the faith. The combined acts of E and I (blue and black squares in figure 4) would place someone in the position of either accepting or rejecting a particular preposition. Figure 4 reduces, to some extent, all actions from 12 to 4, if one follows the squares. The combinations are summarized by the letters E, I, N, and R, which represent the combined acts of the memory, intellect, and will. In spite of its difficulty, Llull's Art had great appeal. It appeared to make investigations into truth more complete.

Llull listed five principles through his Art about God, which he believed were undisputed truths and needed strong consideration. (1) God has his own substantial attributes (sixteen mentioned in figure 2). (2) These attributes are not contrary to one another but are complimentary. (3) These attributes are real. (4) These attributes affirm and should convince that God has aseity, and they point away from his nonbeing (ontological belief of Llull). (5) God's attributes have an effect in this world and each creatures' (human) capacity receives the likeness of these attributes.[36]

Another concept Llull sought to refute using this chart and other charts was the idea of "double truth" that Averroes and other Muslim philosophers promoted. The theory of double truth is the concept that something might be true in theology but not in philosophy and vice-versa. Llull viewed these ideas as a threat to the reliability and practicality of the Christian message among

---

34. Figure 4 is taken from Bonner, *Art and Logic of Ramon Llull*, 93.

35. LLull, *Arte Breve*, 27.

36. Bridger, "Raymond Llull: Medieval Theologian, Philosopher, and Missionary" 12–13.

Muslims that studied and understood the importance of these truths.[37] Llull sought to prove the teachings of the incarnation and the Trinity through the use of the charts. Even the chart of the rational soul emphasized a human life transformed by the infusion of love and grace in this new life. The new inner life displays a superior, incarnate love that overshadows a carnal love, which would make the Christian's definition of love far superior to the "bald monotheism" of Islam. Llull addressed this concept by stating that knowledge of virtues and vices and the application of them in one's life increased faith. He attacked Muslim theology for its radical monotheism because they could not say God was always good since this goodness would not manifest itself until God created the world, specifically, mankind. The good that mankind can achieve would not exist until humanity could exhibit this goodness. A believer acting on these virtues would refute the Muslim claim to eternal goodness based on their strict monotheism. Llull also believed his love for Christ would have never been experienced if not for the incarnation. His love for Christ was the fire that burned deep and kept him going for over fifty years as the mainspring of his being and made his soul long for martyrdom. His proof of the Trinity was the love of God, in Christ, as revealed by the Holy Spirit.[38] Everything God created and made, He made in the likeness of his qualities and characteristics; therefore, Llull's qualities or states of being of the rational soul pointed to God in much more defined terms than any false religion could ever hope to explain.[39] Llull also believed that logic based on actual structures of reality would follow the true patterns of the universe.

THE 'ART' AS A TEACHER FOR THE FAITHFUL

Llull's Art also benefited the believer in reaching truths about the Christian faith and the person of God. The believer would understand and love God, which in turn would assist the believer to turn from vices and gravitate to the virtues described in figure 3. It would even help believers solve life's problems by assisting them to ask the proper questions concerning life. Llull believed his Art was both metaphysics and logic. It was not a body of doctrine but a system; a reasonableness of the existing doctrines of Christianity. It was a technique to recognize and apply the doctrines of the faith. Muslim thinkers in the thirteenth century, including Averroes, had adopted Aristotle's description of God as the *noeseos noesis*, "thought of thought." Even some of the more controversial errant Christian thinkers of Llull's day

37. Bridger, "Raymond Llull: Medieval Theologian, Philosopher, and Missionary," 10.
38. Bridger, "Raymond Llull: Medieval Theologian, Philosopher, and Missionary," 9.
39. Bonner, *Doctor Illuminatus*, 51.

had taken Aristotle's description as an explanation of the Trinity. In other words, the knower, the object that is known, and the act of knowing are one in the same. Llull apposed this analogy, as it would explain away the concept of three persons, distinct from each other of the Godhead. Llull also opposed Averroes' thought of the purpose of knowledge. Averroes believed that knowledge, any knowledge, not necessarily knowledge of God, was to help the common man to action. That is, right knowledge led to right practice.[40] Averroes defined right practice as righteous practice. Llull believed his Art would help the believer have the right knowledge of God and would assist the believer in right living. It was not just any knowledge that would assist the believer in right living. Averroes added that philosophy should not be taught to the common man because philosophy would only confuse him. He believed that philosophy was for the learned who could distinguish between these two truths.[41] He believed the common person should only read the Law (Scriptures) and act on that knowledge.

Llull's work sought to dispel Averroes logic on the two truths theory, which he sought to also prove that both philosophy and theology are useful for all men. Llull wrote in *The Art of Contemplation* that these truths were applicable, no matter how lofty they seemed. He used the character of Blanquerna as an allegory of displaying a good and wholesome picture of the Christian life. Blanquerna displayed the beliefs, or virtues of God, in his life, and Llull is quick to write about this display of affection toward God by this exemplar believer: "[Blanquerna] spoke these words with his lips and pondered them in his soul with all the powers of his memory, understanding and will." Llull describes the rational soul and the characteristics as explained by figure 2, representing the attributes of God, by further quoting Blanquerna:

> O Sovereign Good, Thou art infinitely great in eternity, power, wisdom, love, virtue, truth, glory, perfection, justice, liberality, mercy, humility, dominion, patience! I adore Thee as I remember, comprehend, love and speak of Thee and all virtues herein named, which are one thing with Thyself, as Thou art one with them, one very essence without difference soever.[42]

This quote illustrates how Llull used his Art and the allegory of Blanquerna, and how Llull attempted to teach the Art and refute Averroes, who was very much against any anthropomorphic qualities that humans might ascribe to God. Averroes would not disagree with the basic virtues

40. Averroes, *Theology and Philosophy of Averroes*, 183.
41. Averroes, *Theology and Philosophy of Averroes*, 52–55.
42. Llull, *Art of Contemplation*, 20–21.

of goodness, eternity, greatness, and power of God, but he often disputed or resisted the idea of expounding any other attribute to God by humans, as the human mind understood them. Averroes was adamant that both the Prophet (Muhammed) and God have prohibited the expression of human qualities or attributes understood by human reasoning.[43] Averroes held a low opinion of the commoners' approach to God, apparently believing the uneducated could not approach God in the way a learned man could. He felt the uneducated would only be confused and misinterpret philosophical concepts and should therefore only read the Law (Quran).

Blanquerna was an interesting allegory because it was through this story that Llull used for the purpose of illustrating his Art. In this novel officially titled *Blanquerna: Maestro de la Perfeccion Christiana*, he used the characters to exemplify a Christian life modeled by Father and son (Evast and Blanquerna). Blanquerna was well groomed and brought up well educated, in both academics and in virtuous living. Blanquerna understand what love, family, and faith were, in the Christian sense.[44] The book is made up of five volumes: book 1 being about Matrimony; book 2 concerns religion; book 3 is on the priorities of the Christian life, but in reality is about suffering for the sake of Christ; book 4 is titled the "Apostolic Estate" and is mostly concerned with leadership in the church; and book 5 is on the hermit life, or a life secluded for the contemplation of the faith. The idea was that this novel would act out Llull's Art and demonstrate what the wheels and concentric figures were about. Not only in this novel, but other writings contain the mention of Blanquerna such as the *Book of the Lover and the Beloved* and the *Book of the Art of Contemplation*. The universe, to Llull, seemed largely anthropocentric. He attributes all values as relevant to human existence. He held a huge interest in the soul as he believed each person consists of body and soul. He divided human rational faculties in the traditional Augustinian powers of the intellect, will, and memory.

Llull used much caution in addressing Muslim philosophy and beliefs. He once stated, "The three great currents of this era are Avicennism, Aristotelianism, and Averroism."[45] A central obstacle in medieval religious life is the relationship between religion and philosophy. The Art was supposed to settle all philosophical-religious disputes. One of Llull's contemporaries, Dominican preacher Giordano da Pisa, mocked Muslim law for its emphasis on earthly delights. He was referring to the Muslim emphasis on pleasures of this world, such as Muslim polygamy and Muslim notions of a paradise replete

---

43. Averroes, *Theology and Philosophy of Averroes*, 201–2.
44. Llull, *Blanquerna: Maestro de la Perfeccion Christiana*, 2–16.
45. Hernandez, *El Pensamiento de Ramon Llull*, 34.

with eating, drinking, and love-making. The Christian polemic against such things held that true wisdom despised such pleasures, and sought wisdom and intellectual and spiritual pleasures.[46] Giordano believed Muslim law was irrational. Like Giordano, Llull believed the Christian message was rational and could provide a basis for discovering and believing the deepest mysteries of the faith. Llull's main focus and interest was in the conversion of Muslims and other infidels, and this was the focus of his writings. Llull lived in a time when European scholastics were analyzing and synthesizing ideas of Aristotle and Neoplatonic thinkers, which were preserved and reintroduced to the continent by Muslims and Middle Eastern Christians.[47] Llull vigorously attacked those who sought to put a wall between theology and philosophy because he saw this as an attack on the reasonableness of the Christian faith and he believed this faith could explain deep mysteries for which both Muslim theology and philosophy had no answer for. This protective attitude toward philosophy is why his Art was so important to him—he felt it could explain the rationality of mysteries such as the Trinity and the incarnation. Scott Bridger quotes Fredrick Copleston in his entry in volume 2 of "A History of Philosophy," summing up Llull's life work and missionary and apologetic efforts:

> His interest in the conversion of the Moslems naturally led to an insistence, not only on philosophy's subordinate relation to theology, but also on reason's ability to make acceptable the dogmas of the Faith. It is in the light of this general attitude that we must understand his proposal to 'prove' the articles of faith by "necessary reasons." He no more proposed to rationalize (in the modern sense) the Christian mysteries than did St. Anselm or Richard of St. Victor, when they spoke of "necessary reasons" for the Trinity, and he expressly declares that faith treats of objects which the human reason cannot understand; but he wished to show the Moslems that Christian beliefs are not contrary to reason and that reason can meet the objections adduced against them. Moreover, believing that the accusation brought against the Averroists that they held a "double truth" theory was justified . . . he was concerned to show that there is no need to have recourse to any such radical separation of theology and philosophy, but that theological dogmas harmonize with reason and cannot be impugned by reason.[48]

---

46. Tolan, "Saracen Philosophers Secretly Deride Islam," 186–87.
47. Bridger, "Raymond Llull," 9–11.
48. Bridger, "Raymond Llull," 11.

5

APOLOGETICS TO JEWS

RAYMOND LLULL OFTEN REPEATED Isaiah 7:9 from the Septuagint: "*nisi credideritis non intelligetis*," translated as "unless you will have believed, you will not understand." He was emphatic in linking faith with reason, reminding all who would listen that God wants humans to love him with all of the mind.[1] He believed the great strength of Christianity lies in the ability to prove true its beliefs. Llull reasoned that lofty ideas that needed faith stood on their own, but rational thoughts would ascend to those lofty areas and both faith and reason would meet and prove the high ideals the Christian faith proposed. Llull wanted to reach all peoples, though much of his work was either directed at or inspired by the Muslim community of Southern Spain and Europe. Llull believed his Art could reach anyone, even instruct the believer in correct doctrine.

Some of Llull's thought and philosophy derived from the Jewish Kabbalah. Llull believed that the Kabbalah was divine science and a true revelation of the soul.[2] Llull had an affinity to the Ecstatic Kabbalah, which should be differentiated from the Theosophical Kabbalah. Theosophical Kabbalah was mostly interested in relating the theosophical concept of God based on the ten emanations[3] and the possibility of human action to affect

---

1. Zwemer, *Ramon LLull: First Missionary to Moslems*, 27.
2. Yates, "Ramon Llull and John Scotus Erigena," 39–40.
3. These emanations or "Sephirot" are ten attributes of how God reveals himself and continuously creates the physical and metaphysical worlds. These emanations have changed through time but the thirteenth century version of these would have entailed kingship, splendor, eternity, beauty, severity, lovingkindness, understanding, and wisdom. Two other emanations are more ontological and abstract than they are

the structure of the emanations. In other words, it is more a study into the meaning of "God," which evolves over time. It was also an explanation of the structure of the universe. The Ecstatic Kabbalah, on the other hand, is mostly interested achieving a mystical union with God, which is also called the prophetic Kabbalah.[4] Some believe that much of Llull's Art was similar to the Ecstatic Kabbalah.

The Ecstatic Kabbalah made its first appearance in Barcelona around the early thirteenth century. It was first presented by a prominent Jew named Abraham Abulafia. Llull's logic in an article he wrote in 1305, titled "*Logica Nova*," along with the use of concentric circles follows the same logic Abraham Abulafia used in the Kabbalah. The use of triangles and numbers used in Kabbalistic literature looks very similar to that of Llull's work in his Art. Llull was constantly in contact with important Jewish sources in Barcelona, so it is probable that he had extensive contact with Jewish philosophers and religious leaders and was quite influenced by them.[5] It was these and the greater Jewish population to which Llull directed his apologetic. Some Kabbalists' (Theosophists) were teaching an alternative way to understanding the nature of the Divine Being because their understanding that this divine being had dignities, which were in flux and not static. Like other Ecstatic Kabbalists, Llull held onto the concept that there is no change in the Godhead. He went further into his refutation and explained that God was best understood by these dignities and they did not change, but the diversity of them could only be explained by a triad of agents in the Godhead. For Llull, this was the only reasonable explanation and one could only hold to an unchanging God in this manner.[6]

APOLOGETICS TOWARDS JEWS– JEWISH INFLUENCE ON LLULL

Another Dominican had encountered and debated Jewish scholars in the Barcelona area before Llull had ever debated theology with any Jewish leadership. Raymond Martini (ca.1215–85) was commissioned to debate Jewish leadership on doctrinal issues by the leader of the Dominicans, Raymond de Peñafort. This is the same Peñafort who commissioned Llull to start training centers to evangelize the Muslim world. Martini published a grand

---

descriptive: "Keter" and "Yesod," or "Crown" and "Foundation," which focus the believer on a personal relationship with God.

4. Wolfson, "Studies in Ecstatic Kabbalah," 81–82.
5. Yates, "Ramon Llull and John Scotus Erigena," 173.
6. Hames, "It Takes Three to Tango," 199.

apologetic writing against Jewish theology. Martini also publicly debated with the leading Jewish Rabbi of his day, Moses Nahmanides. Later, Solomon Ibn Adret, a student of Nahmanides, took up the debate with Martini. Martini was commissioned by James I of Aragon to censor all Jewish books around the year 1263.[7] Adret later used Kabbalistic teachings to refute Llull in his disputes with the Dominican. Adret was a leading Rabbi within the Jewish community of Southern Spain and was highly respected. As usual, the common point of contention was the existence of the Trinity and the divinity of Christ. Like Martini and others who contended with Jewish authorities, Llull claimed the dignities of God are present in all members of the Godhead.[8] The basis of Llull's argument was that one must admit that all these dignities were present in the triad of the Godhead. In order to avoid stating that there is change within God, or that God can change, the Trinity explained how the various facets could be present in God. According to Llull's theory, the Trinity is the internal and eternal activity in the Godhead. Harvey Hames best explains this theory:

> To demonstrate this internal, eternal and necessary action within the Dignities, Llull, in effect, invented new Latin forms to convey in that language as well as in the Romance tongues what can be expressed readily in Hebrew and Arabic: namely, deriving transitive and passive verb forms from a noun in order to express agent and patient (i.e., the object doing good and the subject receiving that good). For example, taking the Dignity of Goodness, bonea in Catalan, the correlatives of action would be expressed as bonificant (the agent), bonificat or bonificable (the recipient) and bonificar (the act). The "Arabic mode of speech" of these correlatives of action, as they were referred to by Llull's detractors in Paris, was the key for a Christian reading of God and the creation and would force Jews and Muslims to re-examine their beliefs.[9]

Llull begins his reasoning with the proof that there must be a God who is perfect in all ways and does not contradict himself, nor can He produce evil. This God must be perfect and infinite in goodness, and all dignities must be equal in importance and essence, otherwise they would be mere accidents of nature and not able to exist in and of themselves. Llull also argues that God is a whole unity and logically implies that the triune nature is essential to the ten dignities because they are not just qualities, but

7. Cohen, "Christian Adversary of Solomon Ibn Adret," 50–53.
8. Hames, "It Takes Three to Tango," 200–1.
9. Hames, "It Takes Three to Tango," 200–1.

these make up God's nature and are equally present in all members of the Trinity. This theory is described as the relationship of agent-patient-act.[10] It is also assumed that Llull was in contact and debate with other Jewish Catalan leaders; Rabbi Aharon Halevi (Rabbi Aaron) and Rabbi Ben Jue Salomon (Yehudah Salmon). These leaders, along with Ibn Adret, taught Kabbalistic thought to students, but it was unlikely they would have taught non-Jews. Many assume Llull had Kabbalistic tendencies not only because of the similarities in teachings of the dignities or virtues, but also because of heightened interest in Barcelona on Oriental languages and religions. This heightened interest led many to conclude that Llull had mingled some of his thought with that of the Jewish Ecstatic Kabbalah.

Llull believed his Art was the perfect tool for the conversion of all unbelievers, especially religious unbelievers like Muslims and Jews. In his writings, Llull addresses the issues with the faith of Jews, not attacking Jews themselves. Llull penned his *Doctrina Pueril* to his son to explain the sciences and for him to know and serve God. He explains three types of laws: natural, old, and new. Natural law came before Moses, which was an intelligible law to instruct mankind in morality before the revelation at Sinai. The old law was given to Moses at Sinai. Llull instructed his son that Moses was a Jew and there are many saintly and God-fearing Jews. Then, in Jesus, is a new law, but Jews still observe the old law because they do not understand the significance of the new. They also do not understand the unity that exists between Christian and Jew nor the connectedness they have. It is for this reason that Jews are reviled and despised, although their history indicates that God honored them. Llull was quoted as saying: "They now commit the worse deeds because of their lack of recognition of the significance of the 'new.'"[11] Llull emphasizes that Jews suffer because they hold on to the old law, without understanding the concordance between old and new. They cling to what no longer helps; moreover, they cannot fulfill the old. It becomes a hindrance to their understanding of the new.[12] Llull believed it was easier to debate and win a convert from Islam than it was to do so with a Jew. When it comes to the evangelizing and Christianization of the Holy Land, Llull goes to great lengths to show how easy it is to convert Muslim elites, and by doing this the population will follow. However, when referring to Jews, Llull usually mentions to the general population, and not the Jewish elite whom he felt were men of great knowledge but were unwilling to accept rational thought.

10. Hames, "It Takes Three to Tango," 200–201.
11. Hames, *Art of Conversion*, 87–89.
12. Hames, *Art of Conversion*, 87–89.

EVANGELIZING THE JEWS

Llull was involved in campaigns against Jews in Barcelona in 1299–1300, writing two works: *Canonigo de Lagrimas* (*Canon of Tears*–a writing about a certain synagogue that dishonors and shames Christ but could be honored if it repented and preached the truth) and *Canonigo de Paz* (Canon of Peace–a story of a group of Jews who were stoned by Christians who explained that their unbelief provoked them (Christians). Their belief was that until there was a total conversion to Christianity on the part of Jews, there would not be bring peace and social harmony. Llull was often portrayed as anti-Jewish, but there is no indication from his personal life that this was so. His culture was anti-Jewish. It was common to call Jews "Christ-slayers," but it was a more complex relationship than just mere hatred. The relationship between Jews and Christians was based on theological, moral, and practical issues.[13] Llull referred to Jews as ignorant but not in the way many have interpreted. In *Disputacio de Cinc Savis*, Llull wrote that one Muslim scholar stated that if he could be convinced of the truth of Christianity, he would then convince Muslims who were knowledgeable (in theology and philosophy) to convert the masses who were ignorant of science. *Ignorant of science* was the phrase Llull used to refer to Jews resistance to philosophy–the phrase did not signify a lack of mental capacity.[14] Llull believed it was easier to debate and win a convert from Islam than it was to do so with a Jew. He often gave an example in the Canonigo of a learned Jew who is knowledgeable in Hebrew and a teacher, and if others in the Christian faith could present a coherent argument to him, they might win him to Christ. Giving coherent arguments and proofs of the faith is necessary when preaching to Jewish elite, even if he thought they were not receptive to philosophical arguments.

Many of the Jews of Llull's day were greatly influenced and followed another great Rabbi and philosopher, Maimonides, whose mystical thought captured the imagination of many Jews. Thomas Aquinas had opposed Maimonides earlier in the thirteenth century, arguing that the need for faith could be attributed to five reasons. Maimonides had written that five reasons were needed for faith, but they served not to know God better, but for human perfection. Maimonides' reasons were similar to Averroes' reasons for not teaching metaphysics to commoners. On the contrary, Aquinas taught that these reasons were the very reasons the need to teach metaphysics was great. Aquinas cites these reasons as necessary for faith. Aquinas focused these five reasons, not for achieving human perfection,

---

13. Hames, *Art of Conversion*, 73, 86–88.
14. Hames, *Art of Conversion*, 89–90.

but for a dual purpose of ethical living and a path to God.[15] Maimonides believed these five reasons should be hidden from the common people that Aquinas believed everyone should know and understand. Like Averroes, Maimonides believed these reasons could be misunderstood, twisted, and misused, and might lead an unlearned man to ruin. Francisco Romero Carrasquillo quotes Maimonides' reasons in a philosophic journal:

> (1) The subject itself of metaphysics is too difficult, subtle, and profound for the common people; (2) the intelligence of pupils is at first insufficient for understanding it; (3) the preparatory studies are of long duration and few persevere; (4) the physical constitution of particular human beings is an obstacle (some are too young, others too passionate, etc.); and (5) most people are disturbed from intellectual occupations by their human needs. That these are reasons for hiding metaphysics from common people is clear from the text that precedes the chapter on the five reasons.[16]

Llull excelled in creating a missionary method and vocabulary. He created a preaching idiom in Catalan that both expounded and taught the great truths of the Christian faith (incarnation, Trinity, and Resurrection) as well as a compelling invitation to an intimate and penitent devotion to Christ.[17] Giving coherent arguments and proofs of the faith is necessary when preaching to Jewish elite. Llull's personal feelings were secondary to the primary purpose, which was conversion. Llull refers to Jews as being of dull intellect and having an obscure and crude mind.[18] In *libre de Virtuts e de Pecats*, he blames their incredulity on their lack of utilizing the liberal arts. For the Christian, the *artes liberals* were the basis for further study in philosophy, law, medicine, and theology, whereas Jews put more emphasis in the Talmud for their philosophical speculation. Llull believed that studying the arts would allow one to see the truth: he called on Christian rulers to force the Jews to study Latin and liberal arts so that they would be able to comprehend the truth of the Christian faith. When Llull wrote *Liber de Acquistione Terrae Sanctae'* in 1309, in dealing with Jews he wrote, "Jews are people lacking in science, and when a Christian disputes with them utilizing reason, they do not understand the rational arguments."[19]

---

15. Carrasquillo, "Intellectual Elitism and the Need for Faith in Maimonides and Aquinas," 78–82.
  16. Romero Carrasquillo. "Intellectual Elitism," 86.
  17. Hames, *Art of Conversion*, 77–78.
  18. Hames, *Art of Conversion*, 88.
  19. Hames, *Art of Conversion*, 88, 90.

In *Llibre contra Anticrist*, Llull emphasized that among Jews and Muslims who were serfs, some among them would study the books of the Christian faith that give wisdom and knowledge of that faith. The study of these books would convert many, and in turn, many of those would convert multitudes among their people. However, the study of Christian books was obviously a fear of the immigrant population in Spain at this time, thus the Jewish circles of Llull's day were mostly anti-philosophical. They may have rejected philosophy, but they used its terminology and conceptual framework in their theology and theosophy. Llull believed Jews would convert if they studied his *Ars Generalis Ultima*, which indicates he held Jews were aware of a high level of sophistication in understanding and reasoning. Llull believed that the Art would convince without coercing the Jew into believing.[20] Some of Llull's statements appear anti-Semitic, especially when in contrast, he praises the Muslims for their knowledge of philosophy and being well read people. Llull is presenting a twelfth century scholastic reason or philosophy with Christian truth. If reason is the innate capacity to perceive truth, and Christianity is the only true religion, then Jews are obviously incapable of using reason to come to the truth.[21]

In *Book of the Gentile and the Three Wise Men*, which is considered a great example of religious tolerance of the medieval era, Llull describes an imaginary debate between a Christian, Muslim, and Jew. The debate is a good example of how Llull viewed the Jew; he actually did have a great respect for their beliefs. Each participant in this story is allowed to present his beliefs, with only the gentile (unbeliever) allowed to interrupt and question. The work is divided into four books. Book 1 is the three wise men explaining to the gentile that there is a God, which they prove through reason and logic. Book 2 is the Jew who tries to prove his beliefs are better than the Christian and Muslim. Book 3 is the Christian proving his beliefs are better than the Jew and the Muslim. Book 4 is the Muslim doing the same over the Christian and Jew. In the end, the gentile believes in God and rejoices in the divine attributes and is disgusted by his immoral thoughts and habits. Before departing, the gentile then announces which faith he will follow, but neither of the three wise men are interested in knowing which one he chose. This perplexes the newly converted gentile and compels to ask why the indifference. Given the apologetic nature of most of Llull's writings, this story seems a bit interested in turning this story into a display of the power of Christianity. Llull simply wrote this story to prove that peaceful conversation can be achieved from adherents of the three Abrahamic faiths.

20. Hames, *Art of Conversion*, 92–94.
21. Hames, *Art of Conversion*, 89–90.

Llull seems to believe that his Art, combined with logic, could achieve an understanding with the Islam and Judaism.

The *Book of the Gentile and the Three Wise Men* was probably written early in his ministry because later work was a bit more pointed and critical of these two religions.[22] Llull later wrote around 1300, in his *Cant de Ramon* (*Song of Ramon*) that he believed those who followed these faiths could know the truths through the logic he presented in his works, especially his Art. He wrote:

> New knowledge have I found;
> through it truth can be known
> and falsehood destroyed.
> Saracens will be baptized,
> and Tartars and Jews, and all who have strayed,
> through the knowledge God has given me.[23]

Llull wrote the *Book of the Gentile and the Three Wise* men around 1270. It has been often compared to Roger Bacon's *Opus Majus*, circa 1265–68. One point Llull was successful at silencing Jewish opponents for what he thought was the apparent contradiction. This contradiction was the belief that God created the world *ex nihilo*, yet not believing that God can become human if He so chooses. The belief in one and not the other would contradict the laws of nature concerning God, so both Jewish and Muslim critics were silenced. Llull felt that the Trinity was essential in order to reveal to man the different properties in the Godhead. Because man mirrors his creator, then wisdom, love, and will signify that he is alive, the same must be said about the Godhead.[24]

JEWISH ENCOUNTERS

At one point, Llull requested permission from the king to preach in the synagogues of Spain and to wherever the king's power extended. This request may seem like a highly unusual request, but given that the power was now in the hand of Christians, it was quite common to request and allow it. Llull actually had a debate with a Jew, in Genoa in 1305. Jews were not allowed to live in Genoa and were only allowed to stay there up to three days. The Jew Llull debated was probably a visiting merchant, and according to Llull in his writing *Logica Nova*, Llull had been very convincing, so much so

---

22. Vega, *Ramon LLull and the Secret of Life*, 77–78, 151–65.
23. Vega, *Ramon LLull and the Secret of Life*, 227.
24. Hames, *Art of Conversion*, 206–7.

that the Jew avoided Llull for the rest of his time in Genoa.²⁵ Though Llull's writings resemble Muslim Sufism and are considered a bridge from Muslim to Christianity, Jewish connections are harder to come by, although some, as seen, have strongly suggested Kabbalistic references in his writings.

Abraham Ibn Adret knew and debated with Llull in Barcelona. Llull respected Adret and referred to him by the Catalan term of Mestre (Master or Maestro). Llull believed this man should be well respected despite being an adversary in his debates. It was said of Llull by other Jews that "[he] used to dispute rather frequently in Barcelona with a certain Jew, very learned in Hebrew and a Rabbi" (*valde in hebraico litterato et magistro Barcinone frequentius disputabat*).²⁶ Adret mostly concentrated on refuting Martini's *Pugio Fide*, but occasionally he and Llull crossed paths and disputed Llull's favorite topics, the Incarnation and the Trinity. The rebuttal from the Jewish leadership was somewhat superficial. Usually neither side won, as both used Scripture to defend and attack the opponent.²⁷

Llull listed eight principles of faith by the Jewish character. Though initially criticized for his lack of knowledge of the Jewish faith, Llull was probably referring to the Thirteen Fundamental Principles of faith enumerated by the great Maimonides. These principles are standard for Jewish faith. However, Llull was specifically referring to the eight levels of charity as delineated by Maimonides, which also could also have been a reference to the articles of faith listed by the Kabbalistic work, *Sefer ha-Yashar*.²⁸ A legacy Maimonides left many of his Jewish disciples was the concept of religious language being primarily metaphoric. He believed that instructors of religion understood the significance of the metaphors used in religious literature and therefore they and only they could understand and teach the Scriptures and the logic that came with them. Maimonides wrote in his *Guide for the Perplexed*, "[H]e who wishes to attain to human perfection, must therefore first study logic, next the various branches of mathematics in their proper order, then physics, and lastly metaphysics."²⁹ Maimonides goes to explain, at some length, that many do not achieve completion of these disciplines and therefore are not going to understand their importance. He believes many students of religion will tire of studying and will return to everyday life and its worries. Maimonides goes on to say that common people are not fit for any rational mysticism. In fact, he believed

25. Hames, *Art of Conversion*, 114–16.
26. Cohen, "Christian Adversary of Solomon Ibn Adret," 55.
27. Hames, *Art of Conversion*, 246–47.
28. Hames, *Art of Conversion*, 142–47.
29. Carrasquillo, "Intellectual Elitism," 83–84.

many would trespass and become infidels or just confused on these matters. Maimonides makes the comparison to infants being fed meat, bread, and wine, and would not get the necessary nutrition from an infant's diet of milk and the like. The infant would eventually become sick and possibly die from malnutrition. This was a display of strict intellectual elitism. Maimonides, also like Averroes, proposed a strict faith for the common folks. They can know of certain basic doctrines but otherwise the deeper doctrines must be taught only according to their capacity of understanding.[30]

On the other hand, Llull was enthralled with the topic of divine nature as well as the use of logic for understanding all things divine. Not only did he believe his Art was useful for the instruction of every Christian, but he believed studying the divine attributes gave them the *principia essendi et cognoscendi*, or the essential principles and understanding on God and reality. Llull believed studying the divine attributes gave one a grid or scheme for viewing the world. He adopted the traditional position as stated by St. Victor (1141) that the "human mind descends to the visible by viewing the invisible."[31] Like Aquinas, Llull believed the human mind is varied and some can understand more than others, but nonetheless they all need to start with the basic elements of the faith then grow in their understanding as their faith also grows.[32] This belief was more of a Platonic understanding of knowledge that all humans have. They have the capacity for understanding, but move along on a different pace according to their understanding. Llull believed that God gave humanity this capacity and this knowledge should be passed on to others regardless of their ability to receive the information. Llull did believe there was an obstacle, mainly the inadequacy of the human mind, to understand deeper truths, but he did not shut any off nor did he believe sin had "imprisoned" the mind in sin as Bonaventure had taught.[33] This concept is repeated in Llull's *Vita Coaetanea* and even expanded upon when he writes, "It is appropriate for every wise man to hold that belief which attributes to God in whom all sages of the world believe higher goodness, greatness, power, perfection etc."[34]

As mentioned, Llull argued that the essential nature of God is a tri-unity, since Jews (as well as Muslims) and Christians define God as a "whole Unity." This tri-unity is the substance in which each of the Dignities are displayed and they cannot stand alone otherwise they would be empty and

30. Carrasquillo, "Intellectual Elitism," 86–88.
31. Mayer, "Llull and the Divine Attributes in 13th Century Context," 141, 143.
32. Carrasquillo. "Intellectual Elitism," 92–94.
33. Mayer, "Llull and the Aivine Attributes," 145–46.
34. *Ramon LLull, A Contemporary Life*, ed. Anthony Bonner, 59.

idle.³⁵ Ascribing to God these dignities and believing God is not a tri-unity would make it impossible for a single personality to have these Dignities. Llull writes in *Libre de Deu*:

> And since quantity is an accident, God cannot be a number through quantity. And moreover, because God is infinite and eternal substance, there is no place in Him for quantity, neither with regard to extent, virtue or time. And because God is not consistent with quantity, God the Father, without quantity, produces and generates God the Son eternally and infinitely; and the Father and Son, without quantity, breathe the Holy Spirit through the acts of *infinir* and *eternar*.³⁶

The Jewish response came years before from a Nahmanides (Rabbi Moses ben Nahman). He was responding to attacks from both Raymond de Peñaforte and Ramon Marti and was quite eloquent in defense of the Jewish strict monotheistic position. Nahmanides stated that God has a will without emotion and He is powerful and not weak, but, the term Trinity is completely erroneous given that wisdom is not an accident in the Creator. Nahmanides believed that the Dignities would then add to the number of properties of God. Thus, three properties along with, say wisdom, would then make the number of properties four and not three.³⁷ Llull later refuted Nahmanides' conclusion by using Deuteronomy 6:4, implying that the three names of God appearing in the *shema* indicate a plurality. Not only was this one piece of evidence proving the Trinity, but the implied acts of hearing, understanding, and accepting (belief) are indicative of the three faculties that make up the human being, of which is made in the image of God who is also three personalities present in the Godhead. Adret countered Llull's attack by stating that the mentioning of the God three times only refers to the same unity but three different times to show reverence. Rather than just refuting Llull's logic, Adret used a Kabbalistic explanation. Adret explained that Elohim referred only to the act of judging and leading. And God, being one, is that judge who leads Israel. Addret states,

> And of what the Rabbis said in the Midrash, that with those three attributes (midot) God created the world, with the attributes El, Elohim and Yahweh, know that there are three

---

35. Hames, *Art of Conversion*, 203–5.
36. Hames, "It Takes Three to Tango," 205–6.
37. Hames, "It Takes Three to Tango," 206–7.

attributes; judgment, mercy and a third being a total conjunction (mezugah) of both judgment and mercy.[38]

Adret also responded to Llull's counter attack from Genesis 1, and specifically 2:4, saying it is possible that one name could have been used and that would have been well and proper, but the use of El, Elohim, and YHWH was only speaking of attributes and not persons of the Godhead. Adret is referring to the Kabbalistic use of these names as the essence of God and not in the ontological sense. Adret further states that if the use of three names signifies three persons, then it must, by logic, always mention all three names every time the Godhead is mentioned. Since it is not the case, he surmises that one Unity is present and not a Trinity.

There were many and serious polemic attacks against the Jews during the thirteenth century. They were launched by the Dominican Order and inspired by Raymond de Peñaforte that attacked the Talmud in the 1240s in Paris. As one of Llull's writing titles suggests, *Llibre contra Antichrist*, or the *Book against the Antichrist* (the anti-Christian spirit), combating the antichrist (foreign power) must be with knowledge.[39] Peñaforte encouraged Aquinas to write his *Summa contra Gentiles*, and Ramon Marti his *Pugio Fidei*, which was the most comprehensive polemic tract, which quoted a variety of Jewish sources, both in Hebrew and Latin.[40] The rebuttal from the Jewish leadership was somewhat superficial. Usually neither side won, as both used Scripture to defend and attack the opponent. Adret did not successfully refute Llull's arguments concerning the Trinity, but he did give his disciples and future Rabbis a language to resist the Trinitarian belief and uphold the deeply-held belief in the unity of God.

Two things draw one's attention in the *Book of the Gentile and the Three Wise Men*. First, there is a systematic presentation of the principles of the Mosaic Law and of Islam, with a responsible and adequate knowledge of the contents of both, which was not very common in writers of religious polemic at this time. Second, a narrative tale informs the reader concerning the three systems of belief. Llull imagines that a Gentile, that is to say, a pagan who is ignorant of monotheism, consents to a knowledge of faith through the teachings of three wise men or experts, one Jewish, one Christian, and one a Muslim. After illuminating the disciple upon the existence of a single God, the creation, and the resurrection (truths which all three masters admit), each one presents his own religion so that the listener and the reader might choose the correct one. Therefore, the discussion ends in a deadlock,

38. Hames, "It Takes Three to Tango," 209–11.
39. Hames, *Art of Conversion*, 91.
40. Hames, *Art of Conversion*, 248.

while the Gentile asserts that he knows which "the good religion" is. The *Book of the Gentile* is written in a highly emotive tone, with descriptions of a wondrous, idealized nature, dialogues characterized by extreme courtesy, and outbursts of lofty religious poetry. All three monotheistic religions are well represented, but it is clear the differences would lead to a confrontation of beliefs given the day in which they lived.

6

APOLOGETICS TO THE CULTURE

RAMON LLULL'S WORK AND ministry was largely for the conversion of pagans and unbelievers with the idea that he distinguished pagans as the ordinary, common stock of the population. These included the Jews and Muslims, as well as philosophical atheists. He wanted to reach Christianity's enemies with the truth of the gospel. He also understood that many in his culture, although members of the Catholic Church, were not thoroughly convinced of Christianity's greater truths and could easily be dissuaded from understanding their position in Christ as God's people. Many of his time were nominal or apathetic concerning the truths of God and the great claims of the Christian faith. He believed his Art could instruct these unbelievers and lead them into a greater walk with God.

Llull's conversion, then later his commitment to the Lord, gave him an understanding of why so many had frail spiritual lives and could easily be carried away by heresy and deception from the truth. He consistently demanded faith (belief) in order to understand, but many lacked this belief because they truly had no understanding of the importance this type of wisdom made in everyday life.[1] Llull was convinced of the universality of his Art, and this conviction was a great factor in getting the Art of Arts completed and taught so that many could apply it in all aspects of life.[2] One reason he promoted his Art so vociferously had to do with his desire that Muslims, Jews, and Christians live together under the banner of Christian truth united as the three Abrahamic faiths. He also understood Muslims

---

1. Johnston, *Evangelical Rhetoric of Ramon Llull*, 17.
2. LLull, *Arbol de Filosofia de Amor*, 100.

and Jews were not the only obstacle to this unification. Llull believed that missionary efforts waned because of Christians' inability to logically explain the Trinity. They also could not defend properly, through logic, the Incarnation.[3] Llull disagreed with Aquinas on the proofs necessary to establish the veracity of the Trinity. Aquinas did not think one could prove the Trinity by reason alone. On the other hand, Llull thought this was possible, not only to Muslims and Jews, but to the Christian population of his day.[4]

REASON FOR APOLOGETICS TOWARD PAGANS: UNBELIEVERS AND BELIEVERS

The Book of the Gentile and the Three Wise Men (1274–76) is a work of apologetics designed to demonstrate the efficacy of Llull's method in a discussion concerning the truth or falsity of the three laws or religions of the book: Judaism, Christianity and Islam. The disputants had to be men of good faith who were prepared to follow the conditions of the flowers which grew on five symbolic trees. This dispute or debate involved binary combinations of the attributes of God, the virtues, and the vices, combinations which were related either by concordance or contrariety. For instance, the first tree is representative of God and his essential uncreated virtues. The second tree represents the seven uncreated virtues of the first tree along with seven created virtues. The third tree represents seven uncreated virtues along with seven deadly sins. The fourth tree represents the seven created virtues alone, which further explains them along with conditions. The fifth tree represents the seven principal created virtues again, along with the seven deadly sins. Llull theorized that if the conditions of this discursive game were accepted, then the undeniable triumph of Christianity would come about automatically, without the participants in the debate feeling belittled or threatened. It was the victory of reason.[5] In this story, the gentile knows nothing of religion and is quite sad because of the prospect of death. He recognizes he cannot stop the process of dying, and is grieved by the prospect of an empty life so much so that he despairs seeing these five trees, as beautiful as they are, that he cannot even enjoy their beauty because of the gloomy future that awaits him and all humanity.

To Llull, this gentile represented the culture of his day. The lost who wander without any hope and have no way of logically understanding the deeper things of the Christian faith without someone teaching them. Llull

3. Lohr, "New Logic of Ramon Llull," 27.
4. Schmidt, "Thomas Aquinas and Raymundus Lullus," 123, 129.
5. LLull, *Libro del Gentil y Los Tres Sabios*, 94–95.

does not assign a nationality or specific tradition from which the gentile comes. In another work, he defined gentiles "as Mongols, Tartars, Bulgars, Hungarians, Nestorians, Russians, Ghanians, and many others."[6] *The Book of the Gentile and the Three Wise Men* is written in narrative form and allows all participants to eventually make their case for their religion. Given the hostilities of the day, this displayed an incredible spirit of ecumenism and also presented a challenge for those already in the Christian faith who saw the nominalism of the day. Apathy over religious discourse spilled over to daily life among the Christian population of southern Spain. However, the *Book of the Gentile* ends rather ambiguous without stating which religion the gentile chose. Llull did this on purpose, but as one studies how the gentile was converted and lived his life, one sees which religion was preferred and made more sense to him. This allegory displays a worldview of a benevolent God and the loving nature of his Son, Jesus Christ. Llull wrote at one time, condemning missionary efforts of his day as narrow and ethnocentric. Llull stated,

> [one person said] "Mohammedans think they have all the truth. They must be shown they do not have it." "No," said one of the others, "in this I do not agree. From my experience I believe that comparison creates antagonism. I believe we should show the love of God positively. This is the principle I follow, just to teach Christ. If we make comparisons, then people must defend themselves."[7]

This courteous and gentle approach to evangelism was a reversal of both Peñafort's and Marti's approach of a hard polemic style of evangelism and conversion. The gentile in the story is monotheistic, but Llull makes a distinction of this gentile's monotheism and that of the adherents of the three Abrahamic faiths. Unlike the three wise men of the story, the gentile is not henotheistic (as Llull believed most in his culture were). Each one believes in "his" God but does not deny the deity of the others. Llull believed the religious community of his day, in particular the Christians, were henotheists though they professed to be monotheistic.[8] Llull believed henotheism, tolerant as it appeared, only caused more divisions. It did not teach humans the truth of God but instead was interested in its own view of God, and thereby morphed society into a closed society. True monotheism taught humans about the one God and how to approach him. In other words, it was the life of the believer, displaying God's love and love for God,

---

6. Watson, "Nothing to Gain from the Forest?" 561.
7. Watson, "Nothing to Gain from the Forest?" 566–67.
8. Watson, "Nothing to Gain from the Forest?" 567.

that would be the best missionary effort. Rather than establishing a polite society whereby all may chime in about religious truths, the issues are much deeper and are at the very heart and purpose of Christianity. In the end of the story, the gentile is wiser than the three wise men for understanding this, which is what Llull tried to teach his culture with his great Art. Given the hostilities of the day, there was an incredible spirit of ecumenism, which presented a challenge for those already in the Christian faith who saw the lukewarm theology of contemporary society. Apathy over religious debate trickled over to daily life among the Christian population of Catalonia. The increase of commerce in Catalonia, along with those in the kingdoms of Toledo and Sicily, increased the amount of interaction between proponents of all three Abrahamic faiths. Like St Francis, Llull had aspired to be a "fool" of love for God. It was Francis of Assisi who originally coined the term "jongleurs of the Lord." This phrase comes from French culture for an itinerant minstrel or jester. The inference is that Llull desired to be this jongleur for his Lord, one who was so in love with the Lord that his appearance seemed at times foolish to others, for they failed to understand how wonderful and blessed it was to live in the presence of God.[9] At the end of Llull's story, the gentile gives heartfelt praise to the One God. The lesson being that believing in the one true God teaches men how to pray to God.

Llull, like Aquinas before him, felt that wisdom should guide the believer. Of course by wisdom, he meant the Divine One who not only holds wisdom but embodies wisdom. This Wisdom is none other than the Son of God. This Wisdom would enable the believer to speak the truth and defend against error.[10] Llull however went a step further and wrote to show the believer how to follow Wisdom. Since Wisdom also embodies the Logos, it is necessary to follow his precepts and understand the benefits they bring upon the believer. Both Llull and Aquinas were trying to express what Irenaeus once wrote, that God became man so that man might become what God is.[11] Llull saw a world in which the Creator was not fully reflected but believed that same world should express God in such a way that expresses the perfections of God. Both Aquinas and Llull promoted the "ecstatic" life. For Llull, the ecstasy is not a once in a lifetime phenomenon, but an attitude that remains throughout the life of the believer. Every event in life has its origins or is known thoroughly by God. The point and goal of every believers' life is to be the jongleur for the Lord. Llull believed his Art would help the believer categorize and understand God's ways in his life and would

---

9. Watson, "Nothing to Gain from the Forest?" 567.
10. Aquinas, *Summa Contra Gentiles*, 59–61.
11. Minns, *Irenaeus: An Introduction*, 101–2.

bring the believer in a closer relationship with God.¹² Llull did not write his Art in order to display intellectual capabilities, but in order to bring Christ to the world and the world to Christ. The whole work was written for the unbeliever, whether inside or outside the church. It was meant as a weapon for the battles of life. So much did Llull believe in his Art that when a political religious controversy broke out between the Dominicans and Franciscans, Llull was threatened with excommunication and heresy if he persisted in working formally with the Franciscans. However, he also felt his Art would be lost forever if he did not leave the Dominicans for the Franciscan Order, so he chose to sacrifice and work with the Franciscans. Although he never joined them formally, it was clear they accepted him and he was grateful for their reception to his Art. Also, the Franciscans were more missionary minded at this time, even more so than their founder, St. Francis.

Llull felt that the incarnation could be proven and gave proofs for the incarnation, one of which remains very strong. He stated that every pure power is a pure cause, and God is that pure power and therefore the pure cause. Since the world was "caused" by this pure power, yet the world is not a pure effect, it is clear there remains a pure effect. Since cause and effect are in relation, such a pure cause must be Jesus Christ. This effect, he felt, was every believer's strong argument for defending the incarnation.[13] He also felt that the Trinity offered the same logic. God's goodness cannot be defended if there is no Trinity, his logic ran, because otherwise Christians, and every theist, must assume eternal creation. Because God's goodness cannot be conceived as inoperative, self-communication must belong to the very essence of the highest goodness. Without the Trinity, the highest goodness visible is mankind's and all theists know this is not entirely good.[14] Llull being the "fool of love" and Aquinas' the wise man, leave all believers with a great cloud of a witness to emulate and take into the world.

BLANQUERNA AS AN APOLOGETIC

In *Blanquerna*, the narrative traces the life of its main character, Blanquerna, as he ascends through various sectors of lay and clerical society. Llull's writing has drawn the label of "spiritual romance" because it presents Blanquerna as a sort of Christian hero questing for spiritual perfection, so much so that many thought it was Llull's attempt to "incarnate his Art," that

12. Schmidt, "Thomas Aquinas and Raymundus Lullus," 133–34.
13. Schmidt, "Thomas Aquinas and Raymundus Lullus," 137–38.
14. Barber, *Raymond Llull: The Illuminated Doctor*, 36–37.

is, display what the Art was trying to teach and how to apply it to everyday life. It was primarily a didactic teaching on the Christian life to promote missions to Muslims and the rest of the unbelieving world.[15] Some scholars have thought this narrative is a report on thirteenth-century society, but a closer scrutiny suggests that Llull prepared this narrative through the dramatic linking of this anecdote and everyday ethical principles. These scenes and precepts probably owe very little to Llull's own childhood experience on Majorca, since he wrote *Blanquerna* at Montpellier some forty years later. They depend much more obviously on the general doctrine of moral finality that Llull advocates throughout his work. Following a tradition that extends from Augustine's distinction between *uti et frui* to Anselm's concept of *ordinatio*, Llull assigns to every creature the "first intention," or primary obligation of knowing, loving, and serving its Creator. Applying this single, broad doctrine of moral finality in the representation of diverse, particular conditions of social reproduction requires considerable discursive work. The book *Blanquerna* strives to define a sort of "mixed life" of secular and sacred obligations as the ideal existence for every Christian layperson.[16]

This story rather dramatically displays the use and application of clerical ideals and practices to lay matters, but this job is hardly casual or trouble-free. It was an apologetic for the common man of his day, regardless of faith. Llull believed that each human person was a microcosm. What is meant by this is that in some way, every human reflects the cosmos or the universe. The human being consists of both material and spiritual matter. And just like the cosmos, humans are living organisms with visible and invisible qualities.[17] The human has a unique place in the cosmos because when God chose the human to unite himself to this particular part of creation, He signaled the value and worth of every human being. The human also has a responsibility not only to allow God to work out this salvation in him, but must also assist other humans in their attainment of perfection. Llull stated that the earth, a creation of God, was shamed in that some humans did not honor their Creator. Llull's passion for the practice of getting closer to God and fully knowing him is tied to his objective of converting unbelievers. He believed that the proper contemplation and focus on God would lead one to the right knowledge of God, which would, in turn, lead to right living.[18] This focus is the reason *Blanquerna* becomes such an essential spiritual formation document as well as an apologetic statement. Llull believed that God

---

15. Gonzalez Casanovas, *La Novela Ejemplar de Ramon Llull,* 53–54.
16. Llull, *Blanquerna,* 157.
17. Boss, "Does God's Creation Hide or Disclose its Creator?" 174–75.
18. Boss, "Does God's Creation Hide or Disclose its Creator?" 176.

could be encountered at every point in the unfolding of creation. However, in order to see God, the one contemplating God must first live a holy life. Blanquerna exhibits one who desires to live out this holy life. Because the human is a microcosm, the human must understand God's hand on his/her own soul and understanding his/her own place in nature and before God.

The first twenty chapters of the narrative deal at length with various social, economic, and ethical conflicts that Blanquerna, his parents Evast and Aloma, and his fiancé, Natana, all face in choosing between the lay "order of matrimony" and the clerical "order of religion." Their solutions to these conflicts almost always require some misunderstanding of the power or interests involved. For example, the first chapter describes the background and union of Blanquerna's parents. Their decisions regarding marriage, family, and career offer some obvious, socially ordered distinctions in class and gender as individual ethical or spiritual choices. Evast is the son of a "noble burgher," the heir to a "great household" and "great wealth," but finds himself strongly tempted to enter a life of religion in order to "flee the vanities of this world." Nonetheless, he decides to marry in order to set a good example for other married laypeople and to raise new servants for God. Evast then asks his relatives to find him a woman who is healthy and well-formed in order to produce children of "good disposition," possesses the noble lineage, embodies the resistance to vice, is "well-bred and humble," and comes from a family willing and honored to accept marriage with him. Once Aloma is found to meet these criteria, she and Evast are married, "by God's will." Evast instructs his wife to be an administrator of their household, while he engages in commerce, in order to maintain their estate and avoid the evils of idleness.[19] It is through this lengthy allegory that Llull repeats his three-step apologetic for the believer: to know God, to love God, and to serve God.

TO KNOW GOD

Evast and Aloma are devoted Christians in regard to life in the church, and being a good example of believers. On their wedding day they entered church with very little fanfare and did not dress in traditional wedding clothes, but instead wore clothes signifying their humility, and were accompanied by other devoted saints so that their prayers would be heard. They served the poor following their wedding mass by washing and kissing their feet. They invited these and other beggars to come and feast with them at the wedding. Those who had no need restricted their appetites until they could go home

19. Llull, *Libre D'Evast E Blanquerna*, 5–6.

and eat, not wishing to take anything away from those who had a great need. This demonstration of love and self-denial is how Evast and Aloma began their life together.[20] The scheme here is that Llull is devising to show his audience the virtues of a godly couple, but always with the understanding that the couple knows their Creator and desires to emulate their Savior.

In writing about Llull's three part series on *Blanquerna* (*The Book of the Lover and the Beloved*, and *The Book of Contemplation*), E. Allison Peers states that the aim of this work was "not so much to move the heart to contrition and the eyes to tears as to teach men to love, and teach men to pray."[21] Through prayer and contemplation, one understands fully his God. It may appear odd that it did not occur to Llull to go to Scripture to understand and learn of God in this manner, but this was a highly mystical time in Christianity. Believers were encouraged to use both their intellect and contemplative duties to understand and know God better. Blanquerna later displays this Art of contemplation which helps him understand God better as even Llull himself understood it: "Because he followed an Art[22] in his contemplation, did Blanquerna so abound in the contemplation of his Beloved that his eyes were ever in tears and his soul was filled with devotion, contrition, and love."[23] The *Book of the Art of Contemplation* gives some insight as to what Llull was trying to accomplish in writing about an Art of contemplation. The idea in this work was that a systematic contemplation would enhance the believer's knowledge of God in contemplation his Divine virtues. The virtues should be contemplated in relation to one another, that is, Goodness with Greatness, or Eternity with Power, or Wisdom with Love, and so on. Contemplating these virtues reminds the believer of God's wonders and honor. A person can contemplate all of God's sixteen virtues with his many works whether in heaven or earth.[24] It is obvious by his writings that Llull believed anyone could know God by contemplation and logic. Llull did not deny the need for supernatural revelation, which is why he stressed contemplation and prayer. Through this manner, God revealed himself (much like He did for Llull as he was writing songs for lovers, yet, God revealed himself for him). Llull also believed that anyone could know God through reason. This logic was very much like Aquinas' belief concerning the reason as a valuable tool for the unregenerate to know God. Llull took this belief

20. Llull, *Libre D'Evast E Blanquerna*, 3–4.
21. Peers, *Art of Contemplation*, 5–6.
22. This Art is not to be confused with Llull's Art, but the use of this word indicates this was an orderly, methodic understanding and approach to doing any meditation and contemplation. It is a technique more so than a new paradigm.
23. Peers, *Art of Contemplation*, 6.
24. Llull, *Romancing God*, 63–64.

further than Aquinas, believing it was possible by necessary reasons to conclusively defend the articles of the Christian faith.[25] Reason then is guided by the good intention to know God. His reasons come from his conviction that God's nature and presence can be encountered at any time in creation, through proper contemplation of God.[26] Llull believed that creation was revelation of God and therefore played an important part in understanding who God is. If I cannot see God, it signals that the fall has blinded me from perceiving God. I must therefore seek God all the more to gain a true understanding and vision of the world and who made it. I would then gain wisdom and God would remove my blindfold so that I may see the Trinitarian nature of God through creation. Because the human is a microcosm of the world, in the process of coming to a full knowledge of his creator he must first live a holy life because this goes hand in hand with knowing the God in "one's own soul." Llull tries to demonstrate this full knowledge in the character, Blanquerna, after he had said his prayers and was filled with devotion. Peers quotes from the novel, stating,

> And when [Blanquerna] had ended his prayer, he wrote down the substance of his contemplation, and afterwards read that which he had written; but in his reading he had less of devotion than his contemplation. Wherefore less devout contemplation is to be had in reading this book than in contemplating the arguments set forth therein; for in contemplation the soul soars higher in remembrance, understanding and love of the Divine Essence, than in reading the matter of its contemplation.[27]

Llull suggests that the actual experience of contemplation is much more desirable than reviewing the content afterwards because the experience was an encounter with God and the reading of the notes later only brings back a faded memory and not the exuberance of the moment of contemplation.

Medieval spirituality greatly emphasized nature and the connectedness to God through it. Through the Scriptures, the reader recognizes that Adam was made from the elements of the earth. In their material self, humans will see that as humanity, they are connected to other creatures and given that God took on this same materiality, this connects humans in some mystical way to God. The human being was believed to have been a continuity of the cosmos and in this worldview, all was sanctified by the Creator.[28] Given this belief, it is not a surprise that the Catholic Church rejected any

---

25. Hames, *Art of Conversion*, 191.
26. Boss, "Does God's Creation Hide or Disclose its Creator?" 176.
27. Peers, *Art of Contemplation*, 6–7.
28. Boss, "Does God's Creation Hide or Disclose its Creator?" 178.

research done in anatomy of the human being through dissection for hundreds of years

TO LOVE GOD

In the *Art of Contemplation*, Llull often interjected with his theology a psychology of the human that tied both concepts together, reaffirming what was discussed in the previous section. Llull often used will, that is, the will of the soul and love of God, interchangeably. He believed the will was the most potent of the soul's powers because it directs the human either in the right direction or it led him astray. One of the better explanations from the *Art of Contemplation* exemplifies this thought.

> While the Understanding of Blanquerna reflected, and mentally spake to his Will the afore-mentioned words, the Will replied by asking if it were a licit thing to love nought else save only God. The Understanding answered and said that it might love all things created so that it loved them with respect to God. . . . As the Understanding and the Will of Blanquerna thus discoursed, the Memory recalled how in the Commandment it is said that man is to love God with all his soul.[29]

Just as in his other writing in this trilogy, *The Book of the Lover and the Beloved*, is the central expression of what love looks like when it is lived out. At the very heart of this novel, the author writes that love and service of God is man's very life. He who loves not, lives not.[30] And for Llull, loves central focus, and the real-world demonstration of it, is the conversion of unbelievers. Llull tried to show through Blanquerna how God, being Love, reveals himself and thereby only through love returned can a believer understand his purposes. Llull wrote a great deal about love, especially God's love toward the sinner. He had a strong conviction that man needed to love God in return in order to know and to serve Him. This was not the central reason for man's love toward God, it was so that he might exhibit this love to others. Love compelled Llull to write his Art. Love drove him to the missionary field to seek the lost in the Muslim world. This same love, he believed, should drive the Christian to seek that which is lost; but conversions cannot be done without first having a love for God.

Nowhere is this love for God more prominent than in his *Book of the Lover and the Beloved*. This can be an arduous task. The book starts with a

---

29. Peers, *Art of Contemplation*, 9–10.
30. LLull, *Book of the Lover and the Beloved*, 11.

warning: "Long and perilous are the paths by which the Lover seeks his Beloved. They are peopled by cares, sighs, and tears. They are lit up by love."[31] Much, if not all, of Llull's expression of love comes from his own experience during his conversion. The image of a suffering Christ remained throughout his life and he was willing to be martyred for his Lord as the last and greatest expression of love towards God.[32] For Llull, God exists in an eternal state of good (love) which is expressed in his Holy Spirit and his Son. If the Christian understood the truth of this eternal state, he would have no trouble explaining and defending the Trinity. Love can only be expressed in the boundaries of a relationship, and the Trinity was necessary for God to be perpetually good and loving. If God is a single unity, then love and goodness are rendered meaningless, which goes back to the story of the *Gentile and the Three Wise Men*. The gentile asked the wise men as he posed questions concerning who God is. Bridger quotes from the story where the Christian wise man responds with the quote:

> The Christian replied: "That is not true, for if there existed no distinct personal properties in God, there would be in Him no activity by which, from infinite good in greatness, eternity, etc., would be engendered infinite good in greatness, eternity, etc. For if in God infinite good in greatness, eternity, etc. did not come from an infinite begetting good and infinite begotten good, the flowers of the trees would not be in a condition of perfection, and the abovementioned activity of God's unity would be defective, which activity is infinite in goodness, greatness, etc., and which activity, along with the three distinct persons, each having its own distinct property infinite in goodness, greatness, etc., constitutes the actual divine unity, which is a single essence and at the same time a trinity of persons."[33]

In arguing this way, Llull gives the believer a rational basis for defending the Trinity; however, this knowledge only comes by and through love. At the same time, he offers his own Great Art as an easier, less time-consuming alternative to academic curricula. Understanding how a simplified program of study might seem spiritually profitable for lay people is one of the more intriguing functions of cultural production in Llull's work.

While Blanquerna was educated in this manner in the novel, Evast raised him with fear and love, because all children and youths at this age should be raised and nurtured with these two mores and virtues, along

---

31. LLull, *Book of the Lover and the Beloved*, 23.
32. Bridger, "Raymond Llull: Medieval Theologian" 8–9.
33. Bridger, "Raymond Llull: Medieval Theologian" 18.

with fasting, prayer, confession, alms giving, humble speech and dress, and the company of good people. Evast and Aloma taught many other things like these to their son, Blanquerna, so that when he was older and reached adulthood, he would have, thanks to good customs and nature, a character pleasing to God and to other people, and so he would not rebel against accepting the customs appropriate to good upbringing, which leading citizens and nobles should be the first to possess.[34]

TO SERVE GOD

Llull's *Art of Contemplation* describes what service to God looks like. It starts with pure living and loving God, but virtuous living entails serving the Master. Llull reminds the reader that Jesus Christ gave certain command regarding the greatest commandments. It is through Blanquerna that he states,

> Whence if thou, O Will, wert so great that eternally, without beginning or end, thou couldst love God, thou wouldst be constrained thus to obey His Commandment, for the Lord Who commands thee thus is infinitely good and eternal. But since thou hast a beginning, thou couldst not love before thou wert in being; yet now that thou art, thou art constrained to love, and, if thou lovest not, thou art disobedient to Infinite and Eternal Goodness; for which disobedience He will doom thee to infinite and eternal affliction and torment.[35]

Llull, throughout his life, tried to instill in his pupils the need to be missionary-minded and to do the work of an evangelist. He tried to give Christians tools to equip them for service to God as he was serving God. He did not feel this equipping was just a priestly duty, although he held that office in high esteem. It was the service of all to work in the vineyard of the Lord. The equipping was the object of Blanquerna's life; a life prepared to serve God in the fullest capacity. Perhaps many people of Llull's day were henotheists, believing in their God but never denying the existence of other gods, or it could have been ignorance and neglect on the important doctrines that kept many from a devout life with God. Whatever the reason, at the center of all issues in apologetics was the failure by the general

---

34. Llull, *Blanquerna*, 30.
35. Peers, *Art of Contemplation*, 82.

population from the Christian church to properly explain and defend the concepts of the Trinity and the incarnation.[36]

Llull's arguments were made to attack the misconceptions that both Muslims and Jews had of those topics, but most Christians could not discuss these concepts without stumbling or misrepresenting them. Llull believed one served God by preparing himself for presenting orthodox beliefs in a rational and reasonable manner. Piety and love went together with logic in the presentation of the gospel. Llull believed that the five senses every whole human possessed were instrumental in serving God. This belief may seem obvious to the reader, but the mystical time in which Llull lived debated how useful these senses were in learning spiritual things. Llull had no doubt the senses were not only useful, but because the human is a microcosm, they were avenues to get to know and serve God. Nowhere in Llull's mystical life was there a hint that a human can bypass these sense and get to know God. As he believed that the "eyes of the contemplative are lifted to the cross as a mirror in which the bodily eye and spiritual eyes concentrate their attention."[37] Llull's Art was a reinterpretation of old concepts put into language that all could understand. It appeared radical and even odd, but he tried through logical means to explain important truths so that those of his culture could be prepared to serve and give an account of the hope in them.

Llull taught that prayer was also a good way to serve the Living God. He believed that prayer involved three aspects of the human life. The first was what he called sensual prayer, or a vocal prayer (sensual because one of the five senses is exercised). The second aspect was intellectual prayer, which was based on the virtues of the soul. These virtues are memory, understanding, and the will. The third aspect of prayer was doing virtuous acts.[38] Service was not just a physical act but a spiritual act as well. In remembering the commandments of God, Blanquerna placed great emphasis on the will as an expression of submission to God. In his contemplation, Blanquerna is quoted as asking and responding with his own will and understanding: "While Blanquerna's Understanding reflected, the Will asked if it was permissible to love anything else besides God. The understanding answered that the Will could love all created things if by loving them it might better love God."[39] To Llull, service included alms and helping the poor, as Evast and Aloma did on their wedding day. However, it also involved understanding and loving others as long as all loves led to an increase in love for God.

---

36. Bridger, "Raymond Llull," 23–24.
37. Vega, *Ramon LLull and the Secret of Life*, 56.
38. Vega, *Ramon LLull and the Secret of Life*, 78–79.
39. Llull, *Romancing God*, 103.

Service was not a dry, empty exercise, but an active, growing in the faith and understanding of who God is. Llull believed that an increase in one's love for God would eventually lead one to the desire of martyrdom.

CONCLUSION

Ramon Llull had the strong conviction that creation must exhibit the characteristics of its Creator. If humans were the highest order and made in his image, then there is much responsibility in carrying this out. Humanity must exhibit those characteristics that point to God, especially to those who doubt or who do not know the one true God. Who better to exhibit these characteristics than one who is in contact daily with his Creator and in a loving relationship with Him. The meditation and the seeking of his presence should occupy the thoughts of those who already claim to know Him. Humans should display the dignities of God because they are made in his likeness. Llull believed these dignities were impressed upon every stage of formation of a human's being.[40] Llull believed, as did many medieval spiritualists, that God united himself to the believer, not only metaphysically, but also in a physical sense. God is seen in and among his creation and therefore there is some solidarity between flesh and spirit. Since Adam was made from the soil of the earth, and since Christ became a human, uniting God with flesh, took a different meaning in Llull's time than it does now. The creation of mankind was a reason why the human being is a continuity of the cosmos, or the microcosm of universe. Llull agreed with Anselm, along with other medieval thinkers, believing that sin was dishonoring God and this thought created a militant attitude toward how one approaches God. Llull believed that whoever sins not only transgresses against the commandments, but must restore to God the honor He deserves. This restoration creates an atmosphere of contriteness and even self-denial for the believer who approaches God.

Llull's apologetic to his culture reinforced the need to know important Christian doctrines as well as to understand logic and reason. This knowledge was not in place of moral living but in addition to it. He emphasized the mystical approach as well for the believer. To sum up the culture of Llull's day and how Llull approached ministry to his culture, Ruiz and Soler state,

> But the nature and goal of the work are essentially mystical and orientated towards contemplation. In Llull, however, contemplation always leads ultimately to action, because he considers

---

40. Boss, "Does God's Creation Hide or Disclose its Creator?" 183.

that correct knowledge of God is inseparable from the love of God, that the love of God is incompatible with the failure to render to him, by practical means, all that is due to him, in other words, to do everything possible to convert the 'infidels.'[41]

In his *Llibre de Contemplacio*, Llull not only instructs believers in how to contemplate and go deeper into the knowledge of God, but he instructs them that this knowledge is not only to instruct believers, but to teach and convert those who are in error.

---

41. Simon and Llopart, "Ramon Llull in His Historical Context," 50.

7

EVANGELISM, DISCIPLESHIP, AND IMPACT ON SOCIETY

LLULL WAS A POPULAR author in his day. He wrote in Latin, Arabic, Spanish and Catalan. He tried to reach the masses with his prolific writing and ideas for a new logic. He actually popularized the study of theology by writing didactically and for lay people to learn by heart a précis of the Catholic faith. Llull felt scholasticism was for the clergy, but they had long abandoned any simple method of communicating logic to the common folk; therefore, he devised his Art that would best explain the truths of the faith.[1] He felt that the reasonableness of the Christian faith was its great strength and his Art would be the basis for discovering these truths. Samuel Zwemer, the great chronicler of missionary work, writes with clarity what Llull felt about his Art: "The glory of Christianity, Llull argues, is that it does not maintain the un-demonstrable, but simply the super-sensuous. It is not against reason, but above unsanctioned reason."[2] In order to reach his goal of educating the believers and reaching the lost, Llull dedicated much of his life to missions work. Although he was never ordained by an ecclesiastical body and remained a layman for life, he did go to the nations, the Muslim world to be exact, to do evangelism and bring the light of the gospel to many. Next to writing his great Art, his grand love for missions and setting up missionary training centers were the driving force for him, especially later in life. Llull's missionary journeys included a trip in 1293 to Tunisia, and in 1307 to Bugia (formerly Bougie and Bugia, a Mediterranean port city on the Gulf

1. Zwemer, *Ramon LLull: First Missionary to Moslems*, 56.
2. Zwemer, *Ramon LLull: First Missionary to Moslems*, 57.

of Béjaïa in Algeria). He went also to Kabylia, a port city in Algeria. He was incarcerated for half a year there, then released. He later returned to Tunisia in 1314.[3] As he entered his post-Art phase (1308–1315), Llull focused his attention on the creation of a new logic, conveyed in a series of polemical works during his stay in Paris between 1309–1311. This new logic was not a sudden revelation nor was it a refutation of any previous logic. What is meant by new logic is that Llull was less dependent on his own formulations and more inclined to apply classic Aristotelian principles to syllogisms and was based more on standard academic constructions of his day.[4] Three main works that come out of this post-Art phase were his *Ars Brevis* (1308), *Libre de acquisitione de Terrae Sanctae* (1311), and *Vita Coaetanea* (1311). *Ars brevis* was a shortened version of his great Art, but he felt it was needed in order to explain his major work. The *Libre de acquisitione de Terrae Sanctae* was a strong rationalization of the Crusade to reacquire the Holy Land for Christ, which was quite a departure for Llull who usually discouraged these militaristic events, but he felt this crusade might expedite the conversion of the Muslim world to Christianity. *Vita Coaetanea* was an autobiography given for a couple of purposes. One reason was to make known the reasons for his earlier writings, especially his Art. Another reason was to inspire others to do great things and to do them in an excellent manner. In 1312, he wrote another novel titled *Phantasticus* or by the entire name of *Disputatio Petri clerici et Raymundi phantastici*. Using the Latin term *phantasticus*, this novel is a discussion between Ramon and Pedro. Pedro is a fictitious character who happens to be a cleric who quarrels with Ramon concerning his work and struggles. *Phantasticus* is one of his last works, and it is a dialogue that many believe was a renovation or a reformationist type of writing. Ramon inquires (disputes) why a structured hierarchy is necessary or why it is so rigid in church polity, even becoming outdated and bourgeois. The cleric, Pedro, disputes with Ramon why his Art is even necessary at all. The writing is a bit pessimistic in tone, but underscores, perhaps, his feeling or mood during the last years of his life prior to his last missionary endeavor. Ramon alleges (gently) the clergy of the church to be very worldly and superficial (extravagant). Pedro responds that Ramon barely mentions God's goodness and does not practice or model it as a minister should. Perhaps Ramon needs to start with God's goodness rather than writing about God's other virtues. The conversation goes back and forth, each accusing the other of being extravagant or *phantasticus*.[5]

3. LLull, *Arbol de Filosofia de Amor*, 105.
4. Bonner, *Art and Logic of Ramon Llull: A User's Guide*, 190–95.
5. Llull, *Cuatro Obras*, 187.

EVANGELISM

As previously described, the generation in which Llull lived was a mixture of light and darkness–different than most other times. A deep mystical faith was coupled with pagan superstition. Because he lived in such close proximity to the Muslim world, he became known as the Apostle to the Muslims. He was trained in logic and was quite knowledgeable in the Arabic language. His mysticism was a method of understanding and receiving God's provision for salvation. Mystical belief was never to exalt oneself but was a way to submit to God's understanding of reality. Belief and regeneration was expressed as a relationship between contemplation and action.[6] Llull's way of looking at this process displayed the tradition of the church yet introduced novel language to describe salvation. It is no secret that Llull concentrated his evangelistic efforts among the Saracens, but it was also a difficult time given the hatred for the Muslims from Christian Europe. Christians feared the Mohammedans and vice versa. The failure of the crusades and the destruction of property and life by Moorish pirates reinforced feelings of hatred for Muslims by Christians. Instead of seeing the Muslim as a fellow monotheist of a similar Abrahamic tradition, Christians labeled the Muslims as pagans.[7] Christian propaganda often resorted force or appealed to miracles and ecstasies in order to win converts. Llull rejected these methods, instead settling for a full explanation to the pagan on why Christianity was a rational choice. As noted in previous chapters, Llull believed the divine Logos was the reasonable alternative to any other religious system. Llull introduces the concept of the divine Logos to a method he coined as "the three friends": (1) subtlety of intellect, (2) reason, and (3) good will. These "three friends" would convince any pagan of his error and there would be conversion without the use of force or an appeal to borderline superstitious events.[8] Though Llull was not opposed to human reason, he felt reason alone was not sufficient for an unbeliever to become a believer. There must be the exercise of one's intellect as well as an effort to live morally and devotion to God.[9] Apologist's today owe much to Llull's method, which was due to the age in which he lived. It would have been easy for Llull to rely on the state for the forced conversions then work from there to try to

---

6. Vega, *Ramon LLull and the Secret of Life*, 70.

7. Blackwell, "Apostle of Algeria: Raymond Lull, 1236–1315," 332.

8. Llull was not opposed to the supernatural, as seen in his conversion and much of his spiritual formation, but these concepts were only to be directed by the Holy Spirit and not as a tool for evangelism by Christians. In much of his life he opposed the use of force with the exception of one instance, later in life.

9. Blackwell, "Apostle of Algeria," 333.

educate the new "converts." However, he did not believe this was an effective method and struggled for the right to be heard among the Muslims of his day. Llull held a high anthropological view when it came to soteriology. He wrote, "That religion is the true religion," said he, "which holds the highest and most perfect conception of God."[10] He made this comment applying it to Islam, stating,

> When we examine the Allah of Mohammed, although there be Righteousness and Wisdom visible in Him, there is no Love to be found; but when we examine the Christian Religion we see clearly that in it God is unveiled as Love. Now the conception of God as Love is the highest and most perfect conception we can have of God, and therefore the Religion of Christ is to be accepted in preference to the Religion of Mohammed.[11]

Llull also got in some trouble with the church because of his criticism of Christians given that they were not captivated by the spiritual, moral, and rational understanding of the Christian faith. Llull had a large view of God's love for humanity. This criticism was somewhat unusual for the time and age in which he lived. He not only developed an apologetic for reaching Muslims, but he also set up training centers for other missionaries to Islam, and Llull himself went to the mission field as well.

Llull was actually most successful at evangelizing and seeing conversions of Muslims in his native land of Majorca. Perhaps it was the fear of not converting and living in a land now ruled by Christians, or the method employed by Llull, or the numerous articles and tracts he published while he was there, that brought many Muslims to the Christian faith. Barber explains that for once the "prophet had honor in his own country."[12] As mentioned, Llull's work, *The Gentile and the Three Wise Men*, is a great example of Llull's method of evangelism through apologetics. Llull shines in creating an evangelistic approach and vocabulary. He creates a preaching style in Catalan that both expounds and teaches the illustrious truths of the faith (Incarnation, Trinity, and Resurrection), as well as a convincing call to an intimate and penitent devotion to Christ.[13] Though Llull displays a formidable amount of knowledge of both religions in *The Gentile and the Three Wise Men*, this work was written for what many believe to be an exposition of his philosophy of salvation or a philosophy of redemption.[14] Llull

---

10. Blackwell, "Apostle of Algeria," 334.
11. Blackwell, "Apostle of Algeria," 334.
12. Barber, *Raymond Llull: The Illuminated Doctor*, 44–45.
13. Gonzalez Casanovas, *La Novela Ejemplar de Ramon Llull*, 77–78.
14. Vega, *Ramon LLull*, 74.

stayed away from the obvious discussions one would have regarding the doctrines of Jews or Muslims. He actually pointed out good and affirming truths those other faiths demonstrated. He did expose weaknesses and fallacies in logic that the adherents may have concerning God, but he did it in such a polite and gentle way that the gentile (in this case, an unbeliever in any religion) could not but be impressed how the Bible (not the Christian in the story) taught these truths to begin with. Llull's apologetic was gentle enough to allow evangelism to take place unknowingly, which was how he believed evangelism should be done–not through polemic dispute. In *The Gentile and the Three Wise Men* he takes the reader through metaphoric language trying to describe God's attributes. This book was also an apologetic work structured to further illustrate and explain his great Art. One of the many symbols used to illustrate God's characteristics was the use of trees (branches, leaves, roots, etc.). In this novel, Llull uses five trees to describe divine virtues, created and uncreated virtues, contrast divine virtues and seven mortal sins, and virtues and vices.[15] Why Llull chose a natural motif to explain God, salvation, and a moral life is unknown, but, as suggested in an earlier chapter, Llull was influenced by Kabbalistic mysticism. Furthermore, symbolic icons exhibiting the passion narratives were not widely displayed at this time because Muslim rule suppressed these expressions. Even after the Christianization of Southern Spain in the thirteenth century, the symbols most Christians identify with—the cross, the crown of thorns, etc.—are largely absent. It was not until after the fifteenth century that one begins to see these symbols, this after four hundred years of Christian rule.[16] The use of trees symbolized Christ (died on a tree) or other religious icons such as the Virgin Mary (fruit bearing).

The practice of using natural items to represent religious symbols continued after the Muslims were overthrown, simply because many Christians felt uncomfortable using images or symbols that depicted crucifixion, a bloody cross, or even a tortured Christ. Llull even utilized these natural symbols as substitutes describing the Trinity, the church, and the qualities inherent in each of this important theological concepts. The leaves of the trees are also characteristics used in his Art and these allegorical stories explain that Art. Llull believed that these symbols would assist the believer in his prayers and devotion while simultaneously leading the unbeliever to God, should he use reasonable thinking, and specifically into a worshipful and relational mindset about his Creator. Llull believed nature revealed God and his characteristics. Llull's evangelistic thrust was born out of his desire

---

15. Bonner, *Doctor Illuminatus*, 85.
16. Robinson, "Trees of Love, Trees of Knowledge," 390.

to live and imitate his Lord, Jesus Christ. This desire was not an uncommon among those who sought a deeper, even mystical experience with God.[17] In addition, Llull often used the word *contemplation* in an unusual sense. He did not use it consistently but as a description of the act of knowing and loving God. Llull wrote that Christ was crucified in the center of the earth (looking at a map of the globe this seemed to be in the center of the map) and the cross (a tree) extends across the earth. This visualization should give a picture of God reaching out to man, and no one could miss its significance. Boss quotes Llull as saying, "Just as you have created the sun in the middle of the firmament to lighten and warm the earth, so you have wished to put the holy cross in the earth, to give light to the blind and to warm the heart of Catholics."[18] Giving light to the blind was Llull's central definition of evangelism. Humanity acquires this light by understanding the relationship between nature and humans, and it is through this relationship that one understands the relationship between humans and God.

Llull was quite the evangelist who sought out the lost. During a time of great fear after the Muslim kingdom had been whisked away, another threat appeared to western civilization: the Mongol invasion. Mongols were known as Tartars, and it was rumored that they had invaded and overthrown the small kingdom of Cyprus. Llull saw an opportunity to evangelize and save the Tartars, but when he arrived he recognized that there was no Tartar invasion and the news of Cyprus' overthrow was entirely false. He questioned God's will in allowing him to be misled. Llull used the opportunity to beseech the king of Cyprus to require all infidels and factional types to be present at Llull's preaching on the topic of faith. His purpose was to teach the heretical and dissenters of the Catholic faith, as well as all unbelievers. Although there was no compulsion to attend Llull's preaching, many Muslims, Jews, and pagans did attend and were allowed a time to question and dispute with Llull. These meetings were sadly interrupted by a mysterious sickness. During his stay in Cyprus, he was given two assistants to help him and minister to him. However, these two servants were slowly poisoning Llull. He was removed from the two assistants and went to the southeast part of the island where he was nursed back to health by faithful brethren. He then went into Armenia to preach and teach, but he did not stay long because he found the climate unhealthy for evangelism and discussion on apologetic matters. All this happened between the years of 1300 to 1302.[19]

---

17. Ruiz Simon and Llopart, "Ramon Llull in his Historical Context," 47.
18. Boss, "Does God's Creation Hide or Disclose its Creator? 173.
19. Barber, *Raymond Llull*, 45–52.

Shortly thereafter, Llull traveled to Paris, Genoa, and as far as London, preaching and teaching to anyone who would listen. He returned to Majorca and remained for a period, but in 1306, he traveled from Genoa to Bougie (Béjaïa) on the coast in eastern Algeria. Many believe he was still enthused by the success he had at home in converting Muslims, so his main purpose was to bring the gospel to that part of North Africa which was a Muslim stronghold. He wasted no time in preaching in the city square once the boat landed. His preaching was direct and rather pointed, quite polemic and confrontational. Many historians write that dying for the cause of Christ was a medieval value of many mystics and saints. Llull probably was no different and sought a confrontation with Muslim authorities. Barber writes that Llull preached "The Law of the Christians is true, holy, and acceptable to God. The Law of the Saracens is false and full of error, and this I am prepared to prove."[20] A mob surrounded him and prepared to stone him but the authorities arrived and he was sent before the magistrate, sure that Llull would eventually be sentenced to death through the legal system. However, this part of his life was dedicated to bringing the gospel to the lost despite his many accomplishments in setting training centers to teach Arabic, writing extensively on logic and spiritual formation, and teaching at the universities at Paris and Barcelona. It appeared that Llull had convinced some of the Muslims to convert and had already set some apart for baptism. Though certain leaders convinced the magistrate to behead Llull for crimes against their religion. The magistrate ordered that Llull be expelled and was escorted to a ship leaving for Genoa. Llull somehow escaped that ship and boarded another one just arriving and he was free to roam in Bougie as a new arrival. He stayed for three more weeks, preached and baptized, then headed to Naples.[21] In 1314, Llull traveled to Tunis. Nothing is known about this trip except that he was there in 1315, and that he met with the king of Tunis and even gave the king a letter from his homeland king, the King of Aragon, James II, showing he had support from compatriots. The two kings enjoyed a brief cordial relationship.[22] After this brief period, it appears Llull disappears from history, although there is evidence that this was his final missionary trip. A similar incident occurred as it did in Algeria, but this time he was jailed for a longer period. He was also stoned while on his way to jail, but survived the stoning for a brief time and possibly died on his way back Majorca. The lengthy jail time and the stoning probably took their toll on the aged evangelist.[23]

20. Barber, *Raymond Llull*, 54–55.
21. LLull, *Contemporary Life*, 61–65.
22. Ruiz Simon and Llopart, "Ramon Llull," 57–58.
23. Barber, *Raymond Llull*, 57–58.

DISCIPLESHIP

Llull tried very hard to introduce a militant Christianity. He more accurately tried to continue the work of St. Francis in terms of a deeper walk with God, renouncing all worldly benefits, and do the work of God here on earth. Llull was a reformer, and believed that the church had been hijacked by those in high positions who misused their power. He wrote *Felix*, a story concerning the instruction of believers, to warn the church of the dangers of lukewarm faith. Whereas both the book and the character Blanquerna are concerned with the ideal Christian walk and the understanding and knowing God through righteous and a devout life, *Felix* is more concerned with the salvation (in this case salvation is used as synonymous with sanctification) of souls. Man's failure to love and know God is cause for the world being in its deplorable condition. *Felix* is a call to return to purity and a simpler faith, one exhibited by the apostles and the church fathers. in the prologue of this novel, he wrote, "One no longer finds the fervor and devotion there was in the time of the Apostles and Martyrs, who were willing to languish and die for the sake of knowing and loving God"[24] Felix was concerned with the struggles a Christian faces every day, such as doubt, fatigue, temptation, and fear. The story begins with Felix traveling through a countryside and encountering a shepherdess tending her sheep. Felix stops to converse with her and asks why she is out there alone when the region was filled with wolves and wild beasts who could come upon her and cause great damage. The shepherdess assures Felix that God is overlooking her situation and she is at rest, for nothing happens without God knowing it. Felix is struck by her great faith and moves on, still pondering her words. After some distance Felix hears a great scream and turns to see the shepherdess chasing a wolf that was carrying a lamb away. The wolf then turns on the shepherdess, devouring her and then turns on other lambs making a great slaughter. After seeing this horrific sight, Felix wonders where God was. Did God abandon the shepherdess and her great faith? Is there a God who listens? If God abandoned the shepherdess who exhibited great faith, what about him and his weaker faith?[25] Eventually Felix encounters a Hermit who explains, through a couple of parables, that what Felix experienced was an example of someone who did a good thing. This world, the hermit explains, is an opportunity to do good works. Without this opportunity, the world would be a dark place and might signal that God does not exist, but as it is, He does exist and this is the time and place to do good. Since good is in

---

24. Bonner, *Selected Works of Ramon Llull*, 652.
25. Bonner, *Selected Works of Ramon Llull*, 661–63.

harmony with being, this is proof of God's existence and it becomes apparent that God is the reason the world is good. The shepherdess has gained her reward and is in the Father's glory.[26] Felix is encouraged and begins to once again believe in God and his place in this world.

Through this story, Llull tried to explain to believers that this is what St. Francis was trying to teach his generation when he wrote that the idea of conversion and discipleship was a life of penance, and this type of life should be the goal of every disciple. Francis stated, "Blessed are they who die in penance for they will be in the kingdom of heaven."[27] This was Llull's goal for himself and all who would read his works: a life of penance. This life of penance was where every believer begins his journey in understanding God and understanding his own purpose in this life. Discipleship begins with penance. In *Felix*, Llull tried to guide the reader through the main character's eyes to see the importance of understanding God as a beginning of discipleship. At first, after the hermit explains the shepherdess' fate, Felix resists the notion of this tragedy having any "good" come from it. Could not have God delivered the shepherdess in a more dramatic and miraculous way? However, the hermit explains that one must not fear death. It should be every believer's desire to know God and wish to see him and bask in his glory. A person fearing is not bad, because in fear one understands that God exists. The hermit uses this explanation to prove God's existence. He explains that when one fears he is attempting to preserve his life. The lack of this type of fear would otherwise prove God does not exist since the lack of fear would signal a sense of nonbeing without end. The world would be eternal and there would be no God. Though because he feared, he proved his existence as being more than nonbeing. For this reason, one understands God exists.[28]

This hermit goes on to explain to Felix what is God, the unity of God (explaining a triune being), and the Trinity itself through parables and stories that clarify in the simplest terms these difficult theological concepts. Llull offered these parables for the believer to read and deepen his commitment to God. Through his Art and in his writings, Llull attempted to explain the importance of the divine virtues to the believer's walk and growth. Failure to understand God would create a dissonance and fracture from the believer's lifeline. Where *Blanquerna* was Llull's attempt to explain the importance of the virtuous life as a way to display the virtues of God, Llull used *Felix* to teach and encourage believers who struggled with the problem of

---

26. Bonner, *Selected Works of Ramon Llull*, 661–63.
27. Hoose, "Francis of Assisi's Way of Peace?" 455.
28. Bonner, *Selected Works of Ramon Llull*, 664–66.

evil and suffering in this life. In addition, both *Blanquerna* and *Felix* include the ideal of the hermit lifestyle. Blanquerna's final goal in life is to live the hermit life, a life away from everyday worries, and the ability to live a life dedicated to only God and to contemplate his virtues. In *Blanquerna*, the main character ascends to the papacy but his final destiny and desire is the hermit life. In *Felix*, a wise hermit explains life to the traveler, Felix. Felix has questions concerning God and his goodness, but the hermit always directs Felix back to God and his virtues. In both novels, the eremitic life is of great value and worthy of desire. Perhaps next to martyrdom, no other life experience is valued more in Llull's writings, and in thirteenth-century Christianity for that matter. To a degree, Llull treated discipleship like he treated evangelism–both were approached to get the subject to know and love God. One only has to read about his conversion, and then later his calling into the ministry, to see how he approached the discipling of other believers. In most of his writings, he gives the reader some information concerning the character and qualities of God believing that these qualities would attract the disciple to find more reason to love God.[29]

In *Felix*, in the section titled "Unity of God," Llull explains that God is one God, otherwise if there were many Gods then one God would be superior to others. Llull explains this through the hermit saying that if one God would be more powerful than the others, then that God would be the true God, and all the others would have to obey Him. This idea stressed the unity of God to the believer, by contrasting the discord among humans and explaining to Felix that the reason there is war and struggling among humanity is that man is made in the image of God and therefore mankind tries to be god in this life, but he will never know who God truly is and will never love Him.[30] This theme runs through all his writings. Llull's life swung back forth from the contemplative to the active, so he was not a hermit living only a reflective life. Even as his earlier writing of *Book of the Gentile and the Three Wise Men* was a straightforward apologetic reaching for intercultural dialogue, it was educational for discipling because it discusses how the virtues of God interact with one another in various ways so as to communicate God's dealings with the believer.[31]

In another allegory, Llull wrote to describe the Christian's walk titled *Liber Natalis* (*Birth of the Christ Child*). Six women are the main characters in this story, and they represent praise, prayer, love, contrition, confession, and satisfaction (contentment). Love, of course, is the noblest of these

---

29. Ruiz Simon and Llopart, "Ramon Llull," 54.
30. Bonner, *Selected Works of Ramon Llull*, 670–72.
31. LLull, *Libro del Gentil y los Tres Sabios*, 112–13.

virtues because men know salvation and know God because of his great love toward them. Praise and prayer exalt and adore Christ because in him divinity and humanity are united. Contrition and confession make it possible for men to come to Christ with the proper mindset and heart. Satisfaction claims that the Christ child satisfies the longing of men. This writing goes on to celebrate the Divine eternal being and his virtues, such as goodness, greatness, eternality, power, wisdom, and knowledge. Again, every disciple is growing and increasing in love for the Lord in this walk.[32]

What makes this era of spiritual Christianity so unique was how large numbers of Christian laity were gripped with the exercise and development of the inner life. There was widespread belief that exterior works must be accompanied by interior works in a true display of spirituality.[33] Llull's influence could be seen throughout this century and beyond into the late medieval period.

LLULLISM IN SOCIETY

From the thirteenth century Llull appeared, making a sizable contribution to systemized thought on theological matters. His life mission was an intense piety married to a rigorous systematic method, believing that philosophy played a vital part in the believer's life. He believed in an essential unity of theology and philosophy.[34] He believed faith and reason must always go hand in hand and these two could be used to prove every assertion of theology. In fact, it was the claims of Christianity that affirm and confirm reason, as long as they were presented in the spirit of love. Later in the fourteenth century, after his death, Llull was tried on heresy charges by the Grand Inquisitor of that day, Nicholas Eymeric. Eymeric, whose true intention was to make both the Dominican Order and Franciscan Order into one unified order, brought him up on charges as both orders struggled over which one Llull really belonged to. Llull was brought up posthumously on charges of necromancy. Much of his writings were theoretical and philosophic so there was much fodder for the accusations of heresy. Eventually these accusation came to nothing and by the end of the century the campaign to label Llull a heretic lost steam and the Dominican Order reclaimed Llull as one of their own. Many his biographies were written, and in 1563, and at the Council of

---

32. LLull, *Libro del Gentil y los Tres Sabios*, 113.

33. Kieckhefer, "Land of Lost Discontent: Classics of Late Medieval Spirituality," 82–83.

34. Ballard, "Ramon Lull–Doctor Illuminatus 1235–1315," 213–14.

Trent, it was formally acknowledged that Llull's work was Orthodox. Later, in the eighteenth century, Llull was recognized as Sanctus martyr.

Llull was often associated with extreme and fool-hardy projects, yet his hero status remains strong in his homeland of Majorca. He is often seen as a genius with an extravagant character, much of which is exaggeration. He was a prolific writer but he is best remembered, not for his Art, but for his spiritual devotion and missionary enterprise. The thirteenth and fourteenth centuries were a hotbed of spiritual devotion, and many missionary concerns were born from this devotion.[35] This devotion began as early as the twelfth century with Anselm and Bonaventure, then later St. Francis continued this tradition. It is mostly from Francis, or at least from the Franciscans, that Llull drew his inspiration. During Llull's day, there was a renewed interest in reaching out to Muslims, Jews, and agnostics from the Christian community. There was also sharp increase in spiritual devotion, practices, and mystic readings and conversations simply because Llull's teachings and life-example stirred many to these exercises. Though his Art never captivated the hearts and minds of the Christians, he was still heralded and emulated by many in southern Spain. Llull not only succeeded in starting training centers for language and missions, but he taught several times at what was considered the intellectual capital of the world, the University of Paris. In fact it was at this university that the works of Averroes were banned due to Llull's teaching in logic and theology.[36] Llull's approach to spirituality was not helter-skelter but had order and respected the order that God displays in his creative activity, his expectations of believers to the church, and even in his dealings with mankind. Llull wrote *The Book of The Order of Chivalry* to encourage order from those under the protection of the knights. He makes a distinction between spiritual knights (church clergy and ecclesiastical teachers) and temporal knights. His real target audience was the spiritual knights whose main weaponry was the Word of God. However, as in his call to the spiritual life was both meditative and missionary, so was his instruction to these knights. Llull emphasized that these knights not only should teach, but their lives should display an earnest desire to uphold justice.[37] This writing was an early work of Llull's and already it displayed a combination of the mystical, contemplative life, as well as the practical, missions-minded walk of the believer. It also called for the laity to respect and pray for the knight as this was a soldier in the front lines of the battle

---

35. Ruiz Simon and Llopart, "Ramon Llull," 47.
36. Ruiz and Soler, "Ramon Llull in his Historical Context," 52–57.
37. LLull, *Book of the Order of Chivalry*, 5–11.

for righteousness and justice and in need of prayer. It is best said from Llull's comment in this book:

> Whosoever loves the Order of the Chivalry, it is fitting that just as he who wishes to be a carpenter has need of a master who is a carpenter, and he who wishes to be a shoemaker must have a master who is a shoemaker, he who aspires to be a knight must have a master who is a knight.[38]

Llull was arguing for a social order that Aquinas once suggested–the idea of the believer engaged in spiritual warfare. This of course derives from the Ephesians chapter on the armor of God and preparing for battle. Llull tried to contrast the spiritual from the temporal, as Ephesians was not a call to arms but a call to prepare for spiritual warfare. Like any warfare, this spiritual warfare required training mentally and physically for battle. Llull used these analogies to emphasize preparation before any entanglement with the enemy. It was necessary to prepare and even over-prepare. Llull warned, "Hence, to scorn the training and the usage of that which better prepares the knight to practice his office is to scorn the Order of Chivalry."[39] It was the duty of all, knight and populace, to uphold the order. Llull stressed that one of the most important qualities a knight must have is faith, for without it "no knight can be trained in good habits."[40]

Combining all of Llull's works gives a picture of the man who earnestly desired to change the world. Taken in its entirety, Llull's work displays an extensive range of his life, work, and thought. He was not a scholastic, but one gets a picture of an intellectual, skilled in philosophy and theology. He was a troubadour prior to conversion but became a prolific writer on the mystical experiences of the inner life. He was not nearly as recognized as St. Francis Assisi, yet he traveled into foreign lands to proclaim the gospel of peace and died a martyr. He opposed Averroes Aristotelian philosophy, yet most of his works play out in a Neo-Platonic drama, at least as far as the natural and the human was concerned.[41] His apologetic life was a constant negotiation between Christianity and the other two Abrahamic religions. Llull took to heart the Scripture concerning his apologetic from 1 Peter 3:15: "But in your hearts honor Christ the Lord as holy, always being prepared to make a defense to anyone who asks you for a reason for the hope that is in you; yet do it with gentleness and respect." It appears that Llull followed this type

---

38. LLull, *Book of the Order of Chivalry*, 24.
39. LLull, *Book of the Order of Chivalry*, 24.
40. LLull, *Book of the Order of Chivalry*, 71.
41. Hughes, "Figure of Ramon Llull," 185.

of apologetic method more so than his contemporaries in the Dominican order. Raymond de Peñafort, the grand leader of the Dominicans stressed a more polemic style of apologetics. Llull believed in a more civil method and entered into dialogue with those to which he presented the gospel. Llull honored Christ with his very life—he dedicated it to service for God and chose a difficult task in which to serve the Lord reaching out to a large group of people living within his own culture and home. He believed and taught in thorough preparation as he set up training centers in southern Spain and Europe. Llull was a not abusive nor threatening, but believed in open and sincere discourse with his opponents and the lost.

8

CONCLUDING THOUGHTS

LLULL'S MINISTRY WAS AN attempt to refute Muslim philosophy, and to prove the Christian mysteries of the Trinity and the incarnation. Other theologians and clerics, such as Peñafort, Aquinas, and Martí, had tried before to argue these mysteries but had little success, at least compared to Llull. Llull had an impact in his culture even if his "Art" did not. Llull chose to reach out specifically to Muslims because the Christian world was not sympathetic to Muslims, nor did they try to understand, in large part, their religion. Llull believed, and in some ways proved, that the Christian faith answered all objections to the faith by Muslims, Jews, and pagans. His passion and zeal drove him to start Arabic training centers in Europe for preparing other missionaries to send to Muslim lands. Llull had a heart for the Muslim population since so many lived in his homeland of Catalonia, specifically in Majorca. He actually enjoyed some success in winning converts from the Muslim population in Majorca, and specifically his hometown of Palma.

Llull's work and ministry poses some questions for historians. He traveled much and quite frequently met with popes, political leaders, and other church leaders. He lectured in universities and training centers, and went on missionary journeys to Africa and in southern Europe. He met with kings, sultans, and popes. He was a prolific writer, yet many of his writings no longer exist. He wrote in Spanish, Latin, Arabic, and French. What is questionable about his life is the information concerning his early Christian life–his discipleship and training. Outside of his conversion and subsequent rededication, little is known about what inspired him, and what exactly about St. Francis' life moved him to rededicate his life to Christ so much so that his life often mimicked that of the great saint from Assisi. It is understood that a Muslim servant taught Llull how to read and write Arabic, but who taught him Latin?

Llull wrote to both refute and reinforce; he refuted bad theology and philosophy and was always seeking a way to both teach and affirm vital Christian theological concepts. His *The Gentile and the Three Wise Men* stands as a great evangelistic and apologetic writing of the medieval age. In all, Llull never forgot his missionary task. He was evangelistic in his service even as he wrote to refute Muslim philosophy and Jewish theosophy. He refuted Averroes thought on the singularity or the unity of the Godhead. Averroes believed the Trinity was foolish because God could not be one if he was Three or a Tri-unity. Llull argued that God's characteristics, especially his omni-benevolence, made little sense if he was not a Trinity. The Trinity proved God's goodness and love, for what was there to love before creation? However, a Godhead of three persons exhibited that love and kindness.

Llull was not a polemic apologist. He believed in kindness and winning over both the Muslim and the Jewish populations of Southern Spain. He was respectful of their commitment to their God, believing all were serving the same God coming from the similar Abrahamic tradition. From his early adulthood, Llull was an admired man in his homeland. He was not so much admired but at least respected in areas outside of Catalonia. Prior to his conversion, he was recognized as a brave knight and served in the king's court as a page. He was also well versed in poetry and wrote songs and poems as a troubadour. Unfortunately this also made him quite recognizable as a "ladies' man," which bothered the king. The king had him introduced to Blanca Picany, and soon he was married to this young lady. However, marriage did not stop the young page from his lustful ways. This lifestyle eventually did lead him to an empty life, and he began to see visions of Christ, which led to his conversion. He was better behaved after his conversion, but regressed to his old ways of singing and writing songs and poems, many of which were vulgar in nature. Eventually, at the Feast of St. Francis, he rededicated his life to Christ and it is from that point on that his life is traced (where it is possible) in the work in missions and apologetics.

After his rededication, Llull believed he needed to accomplish three things: die in service to his Lord, be a catalyst in developing training centers for missions to the Muslims, and write a great book to help convince pagans, Saracens, and Jews, of the correct doctrines concerning the One true God. If nothing else, it is known he was convinced of these three items on his life to-do list. Dying for the faith was not a rare desire among the spiritual greats, especially in medieval times. Years before, Anselm wrote how every believer in Christ should contemplate the sufferings of Christ and how to emulate these. Mendicant orders like the Franciscans took up this theme and promoted it to its adherents. It is through these mendicant orders that Llull felt most at home because they often promoted the integration of faith and reason. This age saw Aquinas, Anselm, and the great Franciscan, St. Bonaventure, all promote the importance of the rational thinking and spiritual devotion. Llull bought into this system and integration. Often he was criticized for debating with Muslims using logic and reason and not being more direct using Scripture. Llull concluded that the use of comparing Scriptures with Muslims and Jews would be futile since they also had a high opinion of their Scriptures and considered them truth. There was also the belief that might and force would be a better tool for the conversion of the infidels. Llull rejected this idea. He believed honest and open discussions with both Muslims and Jews were best for a thorough conversion. He believed that once they could see, through logic, the superiority of the Christian Scriptures and God, conversion would be expedited. He believed that the great strength of Christianity was its ability to convince one of the great moral truths. He also had a high opinion of the use of logic in the conversion of the lost soul. He believed the world was lost because of the twisted belief they held concerning God. However, to be clear, Llull was not intent on bringing intellectual knowledge to the lost, but to bring Christ through intellectual, rational thinking on the doctrines of the faith.

Llull first served the church in the Dominican order. Dominicans were the preachers and evangelists of the day. Yet the more Llull served, the more he saw more in common with the Franciscans. He asked to be released from the Dominicans but he was not allowed, even threatened with excommunication, so he never formally left the Dominican order but served with the Franciscans throughout his earthly service. This is one reason why he was never recognized as a priest or friar, but was always a member of the laity. The head Dominican, Raymond de Peñafort, around 1238, encouraged Llull to create training centers throughout Europe for training missionaries in the Arabic language, as well as in other Koranic books, the Torah, and Talmudic writings. Llull was happy to do this, yet he disagreed with the Dominican method of doing apologetics. The Dominican strategy of displaying the errors of these writings and using it as their mode of convincing was not the most efficient way, according to Llull, of reaching Muslims and Jews. Llull believed Christian evangelists and missionaries should know these writings in order to understand these peoples, not for refutation of their Scriptures or holy writings. He believed logic and reason would win out eventually.

Llull was stricken at least twice in his efforts to win over Muslims. He employed a Muslim slave to teach him the Arabic language and for two and a half years, Llull learned through this slave. Eventually, the slave turned on him and struck him with a sword. The slave was incarcerated while Llull recovered from his wound. Then, in Cypress, while debating Muslims and Jews on the island, Llull fell ill only to discover his Muslim hosts were slowly poisoning him. He escaped that attempt and eventually recovered from this attack. He was not fearless as he often told of the first time he was heading to North Africa and was so fearful that he could not board the ship. In every sense he was no superhuman. He was as weak and carnal as anyone else, yet he managed to overcome many of his fears, and late in life, made several journeys into Muslim lands.

The training centers Llull developed taught not only Arabic language, but also Arabic culture. The training centers were holistic in nature, that is, they attempted to be sensitive to the culture that visiting missionaries would be reaching out to. This training was quite an avant-garde method for this time in history. Considering the primary apologetic method utilized prior to Llull's work was force, it can be considered quite a leap forward to do missionary training in this manner. Llull benefitted from these training centers as much of his writings, including his *Ars Magna*, were used as texts for these centers. Through these centers he also teach novice preachers a homiletic method, while teaching the great truths of the Christian faith to students.

In the twelfth and thirteenth century, there was a tremendous increase in the concern of the inner life. Medieval spirituality eventually influenced the thought and practice of the Reformation. In one of his earlier works, Llull attempted to teach doctrine through a novel titled *Blanquerna*.[1] This inspirational writing was to display how the Christian life should be lived. The novel concerned a family who served God by being good subjects of the king, being true to the command to "be fruitful and multiply," and raising a young boy into adulthood. The story then focuses on the young man growing up, and making a decision to not marry his long-time sweetheart but instead to dedicate his life to Christ by living the celibate life of a priest. At all stages of life, it is an allegory of how the Christian life should be lived and displayed. *Blanquerna* was Llull's contribution to his world–always seeking the ideal, always for the kingdom of God. Many researchers of his life have concluded that *Blanquerna* may have been an autobiography set in a fictional story, using the main character to display segments of his life.

The strong spiritual emphasis in his writings and work gives insight into a man who had a high regard for the Scriptures. Another writing, which is considered a part or a continuation of *Blanquerna*, is *The Art of*

---

1. Llull, *Blanquerna*.

Contemplation.[2] This art is full of doctrinal teaching and through it one understands that the focus of the soul should be always contemplating the virtues and applying intellect with revelation of the Spirit as the main source of acquiring knowledge of the Holy. This writing is a not so subtle attempt at apologetics addressing topics such as the virtues of God. He addresses topics like the incarnation, the resurrection of Christ, and the Trinity. To some degree, Llull was inspired by Muslim Sufism and their writings. This sect of Muslims often wrote of God's love for humanity using analogies from the human relationship between a man and a woman. Sufis were often persecuted for their use of this analogy by other Muslims. As a former poet and troubadour, Llull utilized this type of metaphoric language to explain God's great love for humanity, specifically, his people. Llull wrote, perhaps his greatest and most popular novel, the *Book of the Lover and the Beloved*.[3]

Llull may have been saved by fear, seeing apparitions and visions of Christ on the cross, but his devotion and service came from his realization of God's love for him and all humanity. Llull wrote as a scholastic, even though he had no formal training or education after his youth. Llull was also influenced by Kabbalistic writings of his day. He utilized writings from the Kabbalah that emphasized the virtues of divinity (characteristics) to teach and emphasize important Christian doctrines. However, Llull's mysticism was a practical mysticism, allowing him to lead others to the one true God and to personal salvation.

Llull's use of philosophy was never for the inquiry of esoteric knowledge, but as a tool for missions and evangelism. His philosophy was inspired by the gospel and he used it to win souls. Llull desired to show a rational faith the lost could not refute. Even though his great Art was not well received, often in fact, it was dismissed as cumbersome and foolish with its diagrams of circles and tables, he earnestly desired to show why Christianity made so much sense as opposed to any other worldview system. Llull believed the strength of the Islamic faith was its philosophy and he studied and prepared to show the faulty reasoning of Islam. Llull lived in a time of the three great Muslim philosophers, Al-Ghazel, Avicenna, and Averroes. Llull's goal was to expose the false premises on which their philosophy was based and to topple their foundations. To a large extent he undermined their philosophic foundation concerning the big three stumbling block, the Incarnation, the Trinity, and the resurrection of Christ. His hope was not solely to refute, but to show the truth through the use of his Art.

2. Llull, *Art of Contemplation*.
3. LLull, *Book of the Lover and the Beloved*.

It does not mean that some of what Llull did was never without criticism. Some critics believed that he eventually entreated the pope to call for a military campaign to the Holy Land in order to preach the gospel to Muslims living there. Perhaps it was impatience, or maybe he believed a military campaign would bring the matter to serious showdown. However, it was the only time recorded that Llull desired the state to use force in order to facilitate conversions. For most of his life, Llull believed that military action was not the best method used for reaching the lost with the gospel. His greatest opponent, Averroes, was quite the influential figure of his day. He was the one philosopher that had reintroduced Aristotelian philosophy to the west. Averroes' main concern was the human soul and he redefined what Western Culture thinks about the soul, especially after death.

Averroes believed the soul lived on after death, but he never defined what that must look like or where it goes. Averroes believed everything could be taught through demonstration, which contradicted much of his teachings on the soul. Even Muslim theologians thought this was a foolish claim since Scripture and argumentation are also tools to be used in teaching religious truths. Averroes also taught that the human intellect was separate from other faculties of the soul but leaned toward defining this as more of a disposition or an inclination of the human soul. He was never clear, often confusing on the matter of the intellect. He at least recognized the Aristotelian expression that the intellect is a faculty of the soul. Llull did not disagree completely with Aristotle on this concept. Llull though, argued this concept was a reasonable theory, but one that could not be proven in this life. Llull believed that ultimately God was the greatest source of knowledge and only through revelation one could fully understand. Llull made mention that even through these faculties one could not understand a concept like the Trinity, because this is revealed by God. This belief was a slight toward Averroes and other Muslim philosophers who asserted that rational thinking would assist in understanding God and who and what He is. Llull believed rational thinking plus faith plus the gift of special revelation (Scripture, Holy Spirit, visions, etc.) were what was needed for complete understanding. Llull stressed the need for God in understanding mysteries. He stayed away from debates with Muslims that emphasized that understanding alone was all that was needed to truly know God.

Llull introduced his Art to display God's attributes and how any combination of these attributes proves that God is a Trinity. Llull showed that God's revelation of himself through scriptures and individual enlightenment was far superior to any general revelation and his attributes or virtues told the human much more about God the personal being. Averroes made the assumption that general revelation, or human understanding, was always in step with the divine Law. Llull believed divine Law and special revelation were distinct and superior to human reasoning from general revelation. Llull believed his Art was given by divine revelation. His attributes pointed to such a belief. For instance, two attributes, mercy and truth, could show that God revealed himself to those who believed and to those who sought Him. It was mercy that allowed the human to be in God's presence, and truth to see God as He truly is. Llull took to heart the invitation from Isaiah 51:4–6 to seek God because God had promised to reveal himself to those who truly seek Him. Through his Art, Llull contrasted virtues and vices to show their incompatibility and thereby convince his audience that God had no evil side. Muslims do not believe God has an evil side, but their logic and doctrine often leaves one with the false understanding that God is distant and uncaring of petty issues in the believer's life. This distant God often appears cold and detached. Unfortunately, this is the logic used in some of Averroes' philosophy, or at least a logic that one could infer.

Llull's display of virtues and qualities of God could be used to affirm what the Scriptures teach about God. Llull believed his Art described the true reality of who and what God is. He insisted that his Art's purpose was to understand and love God. He also believed this Art answered critics of the Trinitarian Godhead. He was confident all believers could learn who God is through his Art and thereby refute Muslim or even Jewish narrow monotheism. He used his Art through another diagram of how the rational soul interacts through the use of its capacities to understand God. However, one thing Llull believed his Art did accomplish was the refutation of Averroes' belief of double truth, where something true in theology may not necessarily be true in philosophy. To Llull, this double truth was illogical, and his Art, through the use of these combination qualities, would prove it.

Later, this Art would be displayed in his novel *Blanquerna*. The Art was supposed to settle all philosophical-religious disputes. When other Christians were mocking Muslim theology and philosophy for its emphasis on earthly delights, a reaction to Muslim practice of polygamy and their stress on notions of paradise being a place of eating drinking and lovemaking, Llull used much caution in criticizing Muslim philosophy and doctrine. Llull reasoned with both Jews and Muslims that God is perfect and infinite in all his ways, and therefore He cannot produce evil. Llull claimed that the dignities of God are present in all members of the Godhead.

Llull debated Jewish leaders of his day in the Barcelona area as well as in Italy. Llull was often portrayed as anti-Jewish, but this was not the case. The culture of his day was perhaps anti-Jewish. It was common to call Jews "Christ-slayers," but it was a more complex relationship than just mere hatred. Llull believed it was easier to debate and win a convert from Islam than it was to do so with a Jew. He believed that Jews were less inclined to listen to philosophical arguments than Muslims were. Llull believed that studying the arts would allow one to see the truth, and he called on Christian rulers to force the Jews to study Latin and liberal arts, so that they would be able to comprehend the truth of the Christian faith. He obviously believed if they read his Art, many Jews would convert to Christianity. However, Llull also had a great respect for Jewish theology and for devout Jews who participated regularly in their religion. His *Book of the Gentile and the Three Wise Men* displays the respect he had for Muslim and Jew, as well as their religion. Llull believed the three names used in the Shema of Deuteronomy 6:4 implied the existence of the Trinity.

Llull did much of his apologetic directed at his culture, which was either agnostic or just apathetic. One main reason he promoted his Art so vociferously had to do with his desire that Muslims, Jews, and Christians live together under the banner of Christian truth united as the three Abrahamic faiths. Aquinas did not think one could prove this truth by reason alone. Llull, on the other hand, thought this was possible, not only for Muslims and Jews, but for the Christian population of his culture. *The Gentile and the Three Wise Men* is a gentle apologetic that is very respectful and courteous of the beliefs of the three great Abrahamic faiths. He believed the best apologetic to Muslims and Jews was the life of a believer well-lived and teaching others the truths about the one true God. He believed Christians should be *jongleurs* of the Lord, or so in love with their Lord that at times their life appeared foolish to others. He felt his Art was for believers to learn who their God is and why they needed to make him the center of their life. The whole work was written for the unbeliever, whether inside or outside the church. It was meant as a weapon for the battles of life. He believed that the proper contemplation and focus on God would lead one to the right knowledge of God.

Knowing God became a big part of Llull's life. He was driven by the activity of knowing God and making him known to others. He even leaned on his past Kabbalistic inclinations to include nature as pointing to a God who reveals himself. Llull believed that creation was revelation of God and therefore played an important part in understanding who God is. Medieval spirituality greatly emphasized nature and the connectedness to God through it. Through the Scriptures one recognizes that Adam was made from the elements of the earth. In the "material" self, one sees he is connected to other creatures, and given that God took on this same materiality, this connects humanity in some mystical way to God. However, knowing God was not enough for Llull. One must also love God. His *Book of the Lover and the Beloved* displays the yearning of every believer to experience the presence of God is such a way as to benefit from his love and to return love back to Him. Llull was a mystic but his mystical writings were not so lofty or esoteric that they were not readable to the common stock of his day. Llull believed that it was only by love that one could reach out to others with this great love, which was more than just human effort.

This love would lead the believer into service for his Lord. Throughout his life Llull tried to instill in his pupils, and wherever he preached, the need to be missionary minded and to do the work of an evangelist. He emphasized the importance of prayer and its regular exercise and practice. He emphasized the mystical approach for the believer. Llull was an evangelist, missionary, educator, and apologist who took the truth of the gospel to hostile and indifferent peoples. He loved God and displayed this love to his opponents as well as to his students and peers. Llull did get in some trouble with church authorities because he was also a reformer. He criticized Christians for not being captivated by the spiritual, moral, and rational understanding of the Christian faith. The one place he was most successful at reaching Muslims for the faith was in his own home of Majorca. He participated in a revival of sorts as many Muslims heard and debated with him, yet many were convinced of the truths he was promoting. He often affirmed the good the other two Abrahamic faiths were doing rather than criticize. Giving light to the blind[4] was the central definition of evangelism used by Llull. One must get this light by understanding the relationship between nature and humans, and it is through this relationship one understands the relationship between humans and God.

Llull officially died a martyr, but his real contribution was to Christian philosophy and apologetics. He tried to instill in the church a militant Christianity. He promoted a deeper walk with God and called on Christians to renounce worldly things and dedicate their lives to God. He was a prolific writer that used stories to get the truths of his Art across so that these stories would be both understood and put to practice.

---

4. Peers, *Art of Contemplation*, 4.

ABSTRACT

The Crusade of Ramon Llull
Numa Ulisses Gomez, Ph.D.
The Southern Baptist Theological Seminary, 2017
Chair: Dr. James Parker

RAMON LLULL WAS A thirteenth-century Franciscan monk who lived during a tumultuous period in Spain's history. Those who have studied missions believe Llull is the first and greatest missionary to Muslims. He is recognized as the greatest Catalan mystic and poet whose writings helped influence Neo-Platonic mysticism throughout medieval and seventeenth-century Europe. He believed love for Christ and love for the lost should be the only motivating factors to evangelize and teach the lost. Many modern missionaries and historians believe Llull understood salvation by grace in the blood of Jesus Christ. Llull was always in good standing with the church during his lifetime. Chapter one will give an overview of Llull's life, his calling, his missionary zeal, his writings, his apologetic work, and the reasons why he taught the truths of Scripture through his life work. Chapter two will give a historical background and setting for Llull's work and his calling into ministry. Chapter three will explain his theology and philosophy of ministry, giving a panoramic view of his ministry. Chapter four will dig deeper into his apologetic, specifically, his refutation of Averroes' philosophy. Chapter five takes a look at his apologetic work in the Jewish community and evangelism of Jews. Chapter six is looks at his apologetic work within his own faith community, and introduces some of his literature aimed at refuting pagan philosophy in his culture. Chapter seven looks at his travels and missionary journeys and impact in society. Chapter eight will have some concluding thoughts on his work in discipling others and his society.

Llull's aim in his writings and his ministry was the conversion of Muslim and Jews "that in the whole world there may not be more than one language, one belief, and one faith." Soon after his conversion, Llull concluded he should evangelize Muslims, who were numerous in southern Spain. He was inspired by the writings and actions of St. Francis of Assisi who lived earlier, and had reached out to Muslims in hopes of converting many to Christianity.

Llull's apologetic work focused on refuting the philosophy of the Muslim philosopher Averroes. Llull's purpose was to show Muslims the error of this philosophy so that they could not fail to see the truth. The strength of the Muslim religion in the age of scholasticism was its philosophy, and with this in mind, Llull developed a system or logical machine (Art) where theological propositions could be arranged in circles, squares, triangles, and other geometric figures so that opponents could not reject his arguments. Llull exalted the doctrine of the Trinity as central to evangelism, spiritual formation, and apologetic work. Llull believed personal testimony was far superior to any philosophic argument because it testified to the power of the gospel and not to a system. Llull took into account faith and reason as acceptable (in terms of belief) to all three religions. This dissertation explored his spirituality and how it influenced not only his personal life, but also apologetic and evangelistic work.

VITA: NUMA ULISSES GOMEZ

Education

B.S.B.A., University of La Verne, 1992
M.Div., Golden Gate Baptist Theological Seminary, 2006
PhD, The Southern Baptist Theological Seminary, 2018

Academic Employment

Instructor, Golden Gate Baptist Theological Seminary, 2009-2012
Adjunct Faculty, Grand Canyon University, 2011-2013
Online Faculty, Grand Canyon University, 2013-
ministerial Employment
Associate Pastor, First Southern Baptist Church, Avondale, Arizona, 2000-2013

Organizations

Evangelical Theological Society

BIBLIOGRAPHY

Addison, James Thayer. *The Christian Approach to the Moslem: A Historical Study*. New York: Columbia University Press, 1942.

Akasoy, Anna. "Al-Ghazālī, Ramon Llull and Religionswissenschaft." *The Muslim World* 102.1 (January 2012) 33–59.

Akhir, Noor Shakirah bt. Mat. "Al-Ghazālī on the Soul and Its Dynamic Fundamentals." *Hamdard Islamicus* 31.3 (July 2008) 45–48.

Al-Faruqi, Isma'il Raji. "On the Ethics of the Brethren of Purity." *The Muslim World* 50.4 (October 1960) 252–58.

Alwishah, Ahmed, and David Sanson. "The Early Arabic Liar: The Liar Paradox in the Islamic World from the Mid-Ninth to the Mid-Thirteenth Centuries CE." *Vivarium* 47 (2009) 97–127.

Ancos, Pablo. "Los Poemas en Cuaderna Vía del Siglo XIII como Textos Cerrados y Obras Abiertas." *Romance Quarterly* 56.3 (Summer 2009) 154–69.

Anees, Munawar A. "Salvation and Suicide: What Does Islamic Theology Say?" *Dialog: A Journal of Theology* 45.3 (Fall2006 2006) 275–79.

Ansari, Abdul Filali. *Los Mediterraneos: Ramon Llull and Islam, the Beginning of Dialogue*. Barcelona: European Institue of the Mediterranean, 2007.

Aquinas, Thomas. *Summa Contra Gentiles*. Books 1–5. Translated by Anton C. Pegis. Notre Dame, IN: University of Notre Dame Press, 1955.

Arnaldez, Roger. *Averroes: A Rationalist in Islam*. Notre Dame, IN: University of Notre Dame Press, 2000.

Augustine. *The City of God*. Translated by Marcus Dods. New York: The Modern Library, 1993.

———. *The Confessions of Saint Augustine*. Westwood, NJ: The Christian Library, 1984.

Aumann, Jordan. *Christian Spirituality in the Catholic Tradition*. San Francisco: Ignatius, 1985.

Averroes and Al-Mutamid-in Spanish. Films on Demand. Films Media Group, 2007. https://www.films.com/ecSearch.aspx?q=Averroes+and+Al-Mutamid-in+Spanish.

Averroes. *Scientia Graeco-Arabica: On Aristotle's Metaphysics: An Annotated Translation of the So-called Epitome*. Berlin, DEU: Walter de Gruyter, 2010.

———. *The Theology and Philosophy of Averroes*. Translated by Mohammad Jamil-Ur-Rehman. Baroda, India: A.G. Widgery Co., 1921.

Averroës, and George Fadlo Hourani. *Averroës: On the Harmony of Religion and Philosophy*. London: Luzac, 1961.

Ay, R. "Sufi Shaykhs and Society in Thirteenth and Fifteenth Century Anatolia: Spiritual Influence and Rivalry." *Journal of Islamic Studies—Oxford* 24.1 (2013) 1-24.
Badia, Lola. "Estudi del Phantisticus de Ramon LLull. Autonomous University of Barcelona." May 21, 1986. http://ibdigital.uib.es/greenstone/collect/studiaLulliana/index/assoc/Studia_L/ulliana_/Vol026_f.dir/Studia_Lulliana_Vol026_f1_p005.pdf.
Ballard, Margaret Goodwin. "Ramon Lull—Doctor Illuminatus 1235-1315." *Anglican Theological Review* 18.4 (October 1936) 209-19.
Barber, William T. A. *Raymond Lull: The Illuminated Doctor: A Study in Medieval Missions*. London: Charles H. Kelly, 1903.
Barton, Simon, and Peter Linehan, eds. *Medieval Mediterranean: Cross, Crescent and Conversion: Studies on Medieval Spain and Christendom in Memory of Richard Fletcher*. Boston: Brill, 2007.
Basetti-Sani, Giulio. "Muhammad and St Francis." *The Muslim World* 46.4 (October 1956) 345-53.
Beaumont, Mark Ivor. "Early Muslim Interpretation of the Gospels." *Transformation* 22.1 (January 2005) 20-27.
Belo, Catarina. "Averroes on God's Knowledge of Particulars." *Journal of Islamic Studies* 17.2 (May 2006) 177-99.
Belo, Catarina Carrico Marques de Moura. *Chance and Determinism in Avicenna and Averroes*. Boston: Brill, 1974.
_____. "The Concept of 'Nature' in Aristotle, Avicenna and Averroes." *Kriterion* 56 (2015) 45-56.
Beresford, Andrew M. "The 'Mester de Clerecía': Intellectuals and Ideologies in Thirteenth-Century Castile." *Medium Aevum* 77.1 (June 2008) 144-45.
Black, Deborah L. "Averroes on the Spirituality and Intentionality of Sensation. In the age of Averroes: Arabic philosophy in the sixth/twelfth century." *Notre Dame Philosophic Review* (2011) 159-74.
Berkhof, Louis. *The History of Christian Doctrines*. Grand Rapids: Baker, 1995.
Blackwell, Basil. "The Apostle of Algeria: Raymond Lull, 1236-1315." *Modern Churchman* 32.10-12 (January 1943) 329-36.
Blackwell, Ben C., John K. Goodrich, and Jason Maston, eds. *Reading Romans in Context: Paul and Second Temple Judaism*. Grand Rapids: Zondervan, 2015.
Boehner, Philotheus. *Medieval Logic: An Outline of Its Development from 1250 to C. 1400*. Manchester, UK: Manchester University Press, 1952.
Boland, V. "Donald Mowbray, Pain and Suffering in Medieval Theology: Academic Debates at the University of Paris in the Thirteenth Century." *Innes Review* 62.2 (2011) 236-38.
Bonner, Anthony. *The Art and Logic of Ramon Llull: A User's Guide*. Boston: Brill, 2007.
_____. *Doctor Illuminatus: A Ramon LLull Reader*. Princeton, NJ: Princeton, 1985.
_____. *Selected Works of Ramon Llull*. Princeton, NJ: Princeton University Press, 1985.
Borrowman, Shane. "The Islamization of 'Rhetoric': Ibn Rushd and the Reintroduction of Aristotle into Medieval Europe." *Rhetoric Review* 27.4 (October 2008) 341-60.
Boss, Sarah Jane. "Does God's Creation Hide or Disclose Its Creator? A Conversation with Ramon Llull." *New Blackfriars* 85 (2004) 170-85.
Bouzenita, Anke Iman. "Early Contributions to the Theory of Islamic Governance: ʿAbd al-Raḥmān al-Awzāʿī." *Journal of Islamic Studies* 23.2 (May 2012) 137-64.

Braden, Charles S. "Review of the Christian Approach to the Moslem: A Historical Study." *Journal of Bible and Religion* 11.4 (1943) 256.
Brague, Rémi. "Athens, Jerusalem, Mecca: Leo Strauss's 'Muslim' Understanding of Greek Philosophy." Poetics Today 19.2 (1998) 235–59.
Brague, Rémi. *The Legend of the Middle Ages: Philosophical Explorations of Medieval Christianity, Judaism, and Islam.* Chicago: University of Chicago Press, 2009.
Brauer, Jerald C., and Quirinus Breen. *The Impact of the Church Upon Its Culture: Reappraisals of the History of Christianity.* Chicago. University of Chicago Press, 1968.
Bridger, J. Scott. "Raymond Lull: Medieval Theologian, Philosopher, and Missionary to Muslims." *St. Francis Magazine* 5.1 (February 2009) 1–25.
Buijs, Joseph A. "Religion and Philosophy in Maimonides, Averroes, and Aquinas." *Medieval Encounters* 8.2–3 (December 2002) 160–83.
Burns, Robert I. "The Crusade against Al-Azraq: A Thirteenth-Century Mudejar Revolt in International Perspective." *American Historical Review* 93.1 (1988) 80–106.
———. "Immigrants from Islam: The Crusaders' Use of Muslims as Settlers in Thirteenth-Century Spain." *American Historical Review* 80.1 (February 1975) 21–42.
———. "Interactive slave operations: Muslim-Christian-Jewish Contracts in Thirteenth-Century Barcelona." *Medieval Encounters* 5.2 (1999) 135–55.
Carrigan, Henry L., Jr. ed. *Romancing God: Contemplating the Beloved.* Brewster, MA: Paraclete, 1999.
Catlos, Brian A. *Victors and the Vanquished: Christians and Muslims of Catalonia and Aragon, 1050–1300.* West Nyack, NYA: Cambridge University Press, 2004.
Cavazos-González, Gilberto. "Francis, Clare and the Ecumenical Spirit of Assisi." *One in Christ* 46.1 (June 2012) 49–57.
Cessario, Romanus. "Thomas Aquinas: A Doctor for the Ages." *First Things* 91 (March 1999) 27–32.
Chazan, Robert. *Barcelona and Beyond: The Disputation of 1263 and Its Aftermath.* Berkeley: University of California Press, 1992.
———. *Daggers of Faith: Thirteenth-Century Christian Missionizing and Jewish Response.* Berkeley: University of California Press, 1989.
Christian, William A. *Apparitions in Late Medieval and Renaissance Spain.* Princeton, NJ: Princeton University Press, 1981.
Christians, Jews, and Moslems in Medieval Spain. Films on Demand. Films Media Group, 1979. https://www.films.com/ecSearch.aspx?q=Christians%2C+Jews%2C+and+Moslems+in+Medieval+Spain.
Churchill, Leigh. *The Age of Knights and Friars, Popes, and Reformers: The History of the Christian Church from Leif Erikson to Martin Luther (A.D. 1000–1517) Church History Unfolded through Stories That Are the Inheritance of All Believers.* Milton Keynes, UK: Paternoster, 2004.
Cipa, H. E. "The Rise of the Ottoman Empire: Studies in the History of Turkey, Thirteenth-Fifteenth Centuries." *Journal of Early Modern History* 18.1–2 (2014) 184–86
Classen, Albrecht. "Early Outreaches from Medieval Christendom to the Muslim East: Wolfram von Eschenbach, Ramon Llull and Nicholas of Cusa Explore Options to Communicate with Representatives of Arabic Islam: Tolerance already in the Middle Ages?" *Studia Neophilologica* 84.2 (December 2012) 151–65.

Coakley, John. "Gender and the Authority of Friars: The Significance of Holy Women for Thirteenth-Century Franciscans and Dominicans." *Church History* 60.4 (December 1991) 445–60.

Cohen, Jeremy. "The Christian Adversary of Solomon Ibn Adret." *The Jewish Quarterly Review* 71.1 (1980) 48–55.

Constable, Olivia Remie. "Regulating Religious Noise: The Council of Vienne, the Mosque Call and Muslim Pilgrimage in the Late Medieval Mediterranean World." *Medieval Encounters* 16.1 (March 2010) 64–95.

Corduan, Winfried. *Neighboring Faiths: A Christian Introduction to World Religions*. Downers Grove, IL: IVP, 1998.

Coulon, J. C. "Godefroid De Callatay, Bruno Halflants, Epistles of the Brethren of Purity. On Magic. I. An Arabic Critical Edition and English Translation of EPISTLE 52a." *Arabica* 60 (2013) 645–47.

Craig, William Lane, Kevin Meeker, J. P. Moreland, Michael Murray, and Timothy O'Connor, eds. *Philosophy of Religion: A Reader Guide*. New Brunswick, NJ: Rutgers University Press, 2002.

Cross, F. L., and Elizabeth A. Livingstone, eds. *The Oxford Dictionary of the Christian Church*. Oxford: Oxford University Press, 2005.

Cross, R. "Osborne, Love of Self and Love of God in Thirteenth-Century Ethics." *Studies in Christian Ethics* 20.1 (2007) 146–49.

Cruz Hernandez, Miguel. *El Pensamiento de Ramon Llull*. Valencia, Spain: Fundacion Juan March Editorial Castalia, 1977.

Davidson, Herbert. *Alfarabi, Avicenna, and Averroes on Intellect: Their Cosmologies, Theories of the Active Intellect and Theories of the Human Intellect*. New York: Oxford University Press, 1992.

Davidson, Herbert A. "Averroes and Narboni on the Material Intellect." *Association for Jewish Studies Review* 9.2 (September 1984) 175–84.

Davies, Brian. *Thomas Aquinas's Summa Contra Gentiles: A Guide and Commentary*. New York. Oxford University Press, 2016.

Deane, S. E., trans. *St. Anselm, Basic Writings: Proslogium, Monologium, Cur Deus Homo, and the Fool by Guanilon*. La Salle, IL: Open Court, 1961.

De Smet, Daniel, and Meryem Sebti. "Avicenna's Philosophical Approach to the Qur'an in the Light of His Tafsīr Sūrat al-Ikhlāṣ." *Journal of Qur'anic Studies* 11.2 (2009) 134–48.

Debergue, Yvette. "Bonas Femnas and the Consolamen." *Journal of Religious History* 35.4 (December 2011) 532–45.

Díez Merino, Luis. "A Spanish Targum Onqelos Manuscript from the Thirteenth Century (Villa-Amil N. 6)." *Journal for the Aramaic Bible* 1–2 (2001) 41–55.

Doneson, Daniel. "A History of Eternity." *Political Science Reviewer* 38 (July 2009) 5–30.

Eardley, P. S. "Conceptions of Happiness and Human Destiny in the Late Thirteenth Century." *Vivarium* 44.2–3 (2006) 276–304.

Eaton, Kent. "A Voice of Reason amidst Christian and Islamic jihad: Ramón Llull (1232–1316)." *Fides et Historia* 37.1 (2005) 25–33.

Ebbesen, Sten. "Context-Sensitive Argumentation: Dirty Tricks in the Sophistical Refutations and a Perceptive Medieval Interpretation of the Text." *Vivarium* 49.1–3 (2011) 75–94.

Ecker, Heather. "The Great Mosque of Córdoba in the Twelfth and Thirteenth Centuries." *Muqarnas* 20 (2003) 113–41.

Eduardo Marcos, Raspi. "Prácticas, Normas y Consejos para la Buena Crianza de un Hijo: Montpellier, 1283-1285/Manners, Rules and Advices to a Well Nursing of a Son: Montpellier, 1283-1285." Revista Escuela de Historia 1.4 (2005) 255-65.

Egan, Harvey D. *An Anthology of Christian Mysticism*. Collegeville, MN: Liturgical Press, 1991.

Egan, Keith J. "In Quest of the Kingdom: Ten Papers on Medieval Spirituality." *Church History* 63.3 (1994) 439.

El-Hibri, Tayeb. *Reinterpreting Islamic Historiography: Hārūn Al-Rashīd and the Narrative of the 'Abbasid Caliphate*. New York: Cambridge University Press, 1999.

El-Kaisy, Dillon. *Ancient Mediterranean and Medieval Texts and Contexts*. Vol. 9. *The Afterlife of Platonic Psychology in the Monotheistic Religions*. Boston: Brill, 2008.

El-Rouayheb, Khaled. "Impossible Antecedents and Their Consequences: Some Thirteenth-Century Arabic Discussions." *History & Philosophy of Logic* 30.3 (August 2009) 209-25.

Fink De Backer, Stephanie. *The Medieval and Early Modern Iberian World*. Vol. 40. *Widowhood in Early Modern Spain: Protectors, Proprietors, and Patrons*. Leiden: Brill, 2010.

Gaposchkin, M. C. "Isabelle of France: Capetian Sanctity and Franciscan Identity in the Thirteenth Century." *The Catholic Historical Review* 93.4 (2007) 914.

García, Javier Domínguez. "St. James the Moor-Slayer, a New Challenge to Spanish National Discourse in the Twenty-First Century." *International Journal of Iberian Studies* 22.1 (February 2009) 69-78.

García-Arenal, Mercedes, and Fernando Rodríguez Mediano. *The Orient in Spain: Converted Muslims, the Forged Lead Books of Granada, and the Rise of Orientalism*. Madrid: Ediciones de Historia, 2013.

Garciaballester, L. "The Alchemical Corpus Attributed To Lull,Raymond—Pereira,M." *Annals of Science* 48.4 (n.d.) 398-400.

Garrington, Philip. *Christian Apologetics of the Second Century*. London: Macmillan, 1921.

Gaya, J. "Ramon Lull and Lullism in 14th Century France." *Theological Studies* 34.2 (June 1973) 325-27.

Geisler, Norman L., and Abdul Saleeb. *Answering Islam: The Crescent in Light of the Cross*. Grand Rapids: Baker. 2002.

Gilson, Etienne. *History of Christian Philosophy in the Middle Ages*. New York: Random House, 1955.

Glymour, Clark, Kenneth M. Ford, and Patrick J. Hayes. "Ramon Lull and the Infidels." *AI Magazine* 19 (Summer 1998) 136.

Gomaa, Ali. "The Radical Middle: Building Bridges between the Muslim and Western Worlds." *UN Chronicle* 49.3 (September 2012) 4.

González-Calderón, Juan Felipe. "Los Filósofos Naturales del Siglo XIII: Un Intento por Conciliar Fe y Razón." *Pensamiento y Cultura* 14.2 (December 2011) 123-32.

Gonzalez Casanovas, Roberto J. La Novela Ejemplar de Ramon Llull: Interpretaciones Literarias de la Mission. Madrid: Ediciones Jucar, 1998.

González, Justo L. *The Story of Christianity*. Vol. 1. New York: HarperCollins, 2010.

Goodrick-Clarke, Nicholas. "Ramon Lull's New World Order: Esoteric Evangelism and Frontline Philosophy." *Aries* 9.2 (September 2009) 175-94.

Grant, Edward. "The Fate of Ancient Greek Natural Philosophy in the Middle Ages: Islam and Western Christianity." *Review of Metaphysics* 61.3 (March 2008) 503-26.

Halbertal, Moshe. *Maimonides Life and Thought*. Princeton, NJ: Princeton University Press, 2013.

Hames, Harvey J. "It Takes Three to Tango: Ramon Llull, Solomon Ibn Adret and Alfonso of Valladolid Debate the Trinity." *Medieval Encounters* 2-4 (2009) 199-244.

Hames, Harvey J. *The Art of Conversion: Christianity and Kabbalah in the Thirteenth Century*. Leiden: Brill, 2000.

Hamilton, Edith, and Huntington Cairns, eds. *The Collected Dialogues of Plato: Including Letters*. Princeton, NJ: Princeton University Press. 1989.

Hashmi, Sohail H. *Just Wars, Holy Wars, and Jihads: Christian, Jewish, and Muslim Encounters and Exchanges*. New York: Oxford University Press, 2012.

Heckman, Christina M. "Imitatio in Early Medieval Spirituality: The Dream of the Rood, Anselm, and Militant Christology." *Essays in Medieval Studies* 22 (January 2005) 141-53.

Hellwig, Monika. "Bases and Boundaries for Interfaith Dialogue: A Christian Viewpoint." *Journal of Ecumenical Studies* 14.3 (1977) 419-32.

Hillgarth, J. N. "The Evangelical Rhetoric of Ramon Llull. Lay Learning and Piety in the Christian West Around 1300." *The Catholic Historical Review* 83.2 (1997) 318-19.

Hitchcock, Richard. *Mozarabs in Medieval and Early Modern Spain: Identities and Influences*. New York: Ashgate, 2008.

Hodjati, Seyyed Mohammad Ali. "Katibī on the Relation of Opposition of Concepts." *History & Philosophy of Logic* 29.3 (August 2008) 207-21.

Hoose, Adam L. "Francis of Assisi's Way of Peace? His Conversion and Mission to Egypt." *Catholic Historical Review* 96.3 (July 2010) 449-69.

Hope, Richard, trans. *Aristotle-Metaphysics*. Ann Arbor, MI: University of Michigan Press, 1952.

Hughes, Robert D. "The Figure of Ramon Llull (Raimundus Lullus) and the Significance of the Recent Companion Volume to his Latin Works in the Corpus Christianorum Series." *Faventia* 32-33 (2010-2011) 177-88.

Idel, Moshe. "Ramon Lull and Ecstatic Kabbalah: A Preliminary Observation." *Journal of the Warburg and Courtauld Institutes* 51(1988) 170-74.

Ingram, Kevin. *The Conversos and Moriscos in Late Medieval Spain and Beyond*. Leiden: Brill, 2009.

Irish, Maya Soifer. "Tamquam Domino Proprio: Contesting Ecclesiastical Lordship over Jews in Thirteenth-Century Castile." *Medieval Encounters* 19.5 (December 2013) 534-66.

Jamil-Ur-Behman, Mohammad, trans. *The Philosophy and Theology of Averroes*. Baroda, India: A.G. Widgery, 1921.

Johnson, Alan F. "The Historical-Critical Method: Egyptian Gold or Pagan Precipice." *Journal of the Evangelical Theological Society* 26.1 (March 1983) 3-15.

Johnston, Mark D. *The Evangelical Rhetoric of Ramon LLull; Lay Learning and Piety in the Christian West Around 1300*. New York: Oxford Press, 1996.

Jordan, E. L. "Roving Nuns and Cistercian Realities: The Cloistering of Religious Women in the Thirteenth Century." *Journal of Medieval and Early Modern Studies* 42.3 (2012) 597-614.

Jung, Jacqueline E. "Judaism and Christian Art: Aesthetic Anxieties from the Catacombs to Colonialism/The Jew, the Cathedral, and the Medieval City: Synagoga and Ecclesia in the Thirteenth Century." *Art Bulletin* 95.3 (September 2013) 488-93.

Khan, Ayaz. "Human Ignorance (Jahiliyyah) Past & Present." *Dialogue Academic Journal* 8.4 (October 2013) 346–59.
Kahn, David. "On the Origin of Polyalphabetic Substitution." *Isis* 71.1 (1980) 122–27.
Kamen, Henry. *The Spanish Inquisition: A Historical Revision.* New Haven: Yale University Press, 2014.
Kars, Aydogan. "Two Modes of Unsaying in the Early Thirteenth Century Islamic Lands: Theorizing Apophasis through Maimonides and Ibn 'Arabi." *International Journal for Philosophy of Religion* 74.3 (December 2013) 261–78.
Kempf, Friedrich. *The Church in the Age of Feudalism.* New York: Seabury, 1980.
Keyes, Frances Parkinson. *Tongues of Fire.* New York: Coward McCan, 1996.
Kieckhefer, Richard. "The Land of Lost Discontent: Classics of Late Medieval Spirituality." *The Journal of Religion* 72 (1992) 82–88.
La Disgregacíon Del Islam Andalusí Y El Avance Cristiano—in Spanish. Films on Demand. Films Media Group, 2004. https://www.films.com/ecSearch.aspx?q=La+Disgregacion+Del+Islam+Andalusi+Y+El+Avance+Cristiano.
Laato, Antti, and Pekka Lindqvist. *Encounters of the Children of Abraham from Ancient to Modern Times.* Leiden: Brill, 2010.
Lachter, Hartley. "The Politics of Secrets: Thirteenth-Century Kabbalah in Context." *Jewish Quarterly Review* 101.4 (2011) 502–10.
Landolt, Hermann, and Todd Lawson. *Reason and Inspiration in Islam: Theology, Philosophy and Mysticism in Muslim Thought—Essays in Honour of Hermann Landolt.* London; I.B. Tauris, 2005.
La Época De Las Calamidades—in Spanish with English Subtitles. Films on Demand. Films Media Group, 2004. https://www.films.com/ecSearch.aspx?q=La+Epoca+De+Las+Calamidades.
Lawler, Peter Augustine. "The Logos in Western Thought." *Modern Age* 51.1 (Winter 2009) 42–46.
Lerner, Robert E. "The Uses of Heterodoxy: The French Monarchy and Unbelief in the Thirteenth Century." *French Historical Studies* 4.2 (1965) 189–202.
Levi ben Gershom, and Menachem Marc Kellner. *Commentary on Song of Songs.* New Haven: Yale University Press, 1998.
Linehan, Peter. *The Spanish Church and the Papacy in the Thirteenth Century.* Cambridge, England: University Press, 1971.
LLull, Ramon. *Arbol de Filosofia de Amor.* Edited by Albert Sanchez Nieto and Jordi Fernandez Pardo. Barcelona: Millenium Liber, 2014.
———. *The Art of Contemplation.* Translated by Edgar Allison Peers. London: Society for Promoting Christian Knowledge, 1925.
———. *Arte Breve.* Translated by Josep E. Rubio. Pamplona, Spain. Ediciones Universidad de Navarra, 2004.
———. *Blanquerna.* Edited by Albert Soler. Barcelona. Editorial Barcino. 1995.
———. *Blanquerna: Maestro de la Perfeccion Christiana en los Estados de Matrimonio, Religion, Prelacia, Apostolico Señorio y Vida Eremitica.* Reprint, Valencia: Impresoria Real Audencia, 1923.
———. *The Book of the Lover and the Beloved.* Translated by Edgar Allison Peers. New York: MacMillan, 1923.
———. *The Book of the Order of Chivalry.* Translated by Noel Fallows. Woodbridge Suffolk, UK: Boydell, 2013.

———. *A Contemporary Life*. Edited by Anthony Bonner. Barcelona: Barcino-Tamesis, 1985.

———. *A Contemporary Life*. Edited by Anthony Bonner. Princeton: Princeton University Press, 1993.

———. *Cuatro Obras Lo Desconort, Canto de Ramon, Liber Natalis, Phantasticus*. Edited by Matilda Rovira Soler. Madrid: Ediciones Atenea, 2013.

———. *Disputa del Clergue Pere de Ramon, el Fantastic*. Barcelona: Universitat de Barcelona, Spain. Publicaciones, 1985.

———. *Disputa Entre la Fe I L'Enteniment*. Edited by Josep Batalla and Alexander Fidora. Santa Coloma de Queralt, Spain: Brepols. 2011.

———. *Libre D'Evast E Blanquerna*. Barcelona: Impres a Grafiques Instar, 1982.

———. *Libro del Gentil y los Tres Sabios*. Translated by Matilde Conde Salazar. Madrid: Universidad Nacional de Educacion a Distancia, 2015.

———. *Romancing God*. Edited by Henry L. Carrigan, Jr. Brewster, MA: Paraclete, 1999.

Lohr, Charles. "The New Logic of Ramon Llull." *Enrahonar* 18 (1992) 23–35.

Lomba, Joaquin. "La Imaginación en Avempace." *Tópicos. Revista De Filosofía* no. 29 (December 2005) 157–69.

Magnier, Grace. *Pedro de Valencia and the Catholic Apologists of the Expulsion of the Moriscos: Visions of Christianity and Kingship*. Boston: Brill, 2010.

Mallett, Alex. "The Life of Aq-Sunqur al-Bursuqi: Some Notes on Twelfth-Century Islamic History and Thirteenth-Century Muslim Historiography." *Turkish Historical Review* 2.1 (May 2011) 39–56.

Marenbon, John. *The Oxford Handbook of Medieval Philosophy*. New York: Oxford University Press, 2012.

Marrone, Steven P. *The Light of Thy Countenance: Science and Knowledge of God in the Thirteenth Century*. Boston: Brill, 2001.

Mayer, Annemarie C. "Llull and the Divine Attributes in 13th Century Context." *Anuario Filosofico* 49.1 (January 2016) 139–54.

McBeth, Leon. *Men Who Made Missions*. Nashville: Broadman, 1967.

McCarthy, Joseph M. "Ramon Llull and the Teaching of Foreign Languages in the Late Middle Ages." Paper presented at the Suffolk University College of Arts and Sciences Faculty Research Seminar (2010) 1–13.

McCurry, Don M. "Cross-Cultural Models for Muslim Evangelism." *Missiology* 4.3 (July 1976) 267–83.

McVey, Chrys. "The Land of Unlikeness: The Risk and Promise of Muslim-Christian Dialogue." *New Blackfriars* 89.1022 (July 2008) 369–84

Melamed, Abraham. "The Myth of the Jewish Origins of Philosophy in the Renaissance: from Aristotle to Plato." *Jewish History* 26.1/2 (February 2012) 41–59.

Meyer, Hannah. "Making Sense of Christian Excommunication of Jews in Thirteenth-Century England." *Jewish Quarterly Review* 100.4 (2010) 598–630.

Meyerson, Mark D. *Jews in an Iberian Frontier Kingdom: Society, Economy, and Politics in Morvedre, 1248–1391*. Leiden: Brill, 2004.

Minns, Denis. *Irenaeus: An Introduction*. New York: T & T Clark, 2010.

Mohammed, Ovey N. *Averroes' Doctrine of Immortality: A Matter of Controversy*. Waterloo, Ontario: Published for the Canadian Corp. for Studies in Religion/Corporation Canadienne des Sciences Religieuses by Wilfrid Laurier University Press, 1984.

Moini, Qasim A. "The Ethical Ideal." *Hamdard Islamicus* 36.3 (July 2013) 97.
Moreland, J. P., and William Lane Craig, eds. *Philosophical Foundations for Christian Worldview*. Downers Grove, IL: InterVarsity, 2003.
Montgomery, John Warwick. "Computer Origins and the Defense of the Faith." *Journal of Perspectives and Science* 56.3 (2004) 189–92.
Moosa, E. "Translating Neuroethics: Reflections from Muslim Ethics Commentary on Ethical Concepts and Future Challenges of Neuroimaging: An Islamic Perspective." *Science and Engineering Ethics* 18.3 (2012) 519–28.
Morris, James W. "Imaging Islam: Intellect and Imagination in Islamic Philosophy, Poetry, and Painting." *Religion & the Arts* 12.1–3 (March 2008) 294–318.
Moses Paul. *The Saint and the Sultan: The Crusades, Islam, and Francis of Assisi's Mission of Peace*. New York: Doubleday Religion, 2009.
Mutluel, Osman1. "İslam Estetiğine Genel Bir Yaklaşim." *Journal of Academic Studies* 14.52 (February 2012) 35–54.
Najjar, Fauzi M. "Al-Farabi's Harmonization of Plato's and Aristotle'sPhilosophies." *Muslim World* 94.1 (January 2004) 29–44.
Nair, Shankar Ayillath. "Philosophy in Any Language: Interaction between Arabic, Sanskrit, and Persian Intellectual Cultures in Mughal South Asia." Ph.D. diss., Harvard University, 2014.
Netland, Harold A. *Dissonant Voices: Religious Pluralism and the Question of Truth*. Grand Rapids: Eerdmans, 1991.
Newhall, Richard Ager. *The Crusades*. New York: Holt, Rinehart and Winston, 1963.
Nowviskie, Bethany Paige. "Speculative Computing: Instruments for Interpretive Scholarship." Ph.D. diss., University of Virginia, 2004.
Nuland, Sherwin B. *Maimonides*. New York: Nextbook, 2005.
O'Connor, Isabel A. "Muslim Mudejar Women in Thirteenth-Century Spain: Dispelling the Stereotypes." *Journal of Muslim Minority Affairs* 27.1 (April 2007) 55–70.
O'Donoghue, Heather. "Poetry on Christian Subjects, I: The Twelfth and Thirteenth Centuries; II: The Fourteenth Century/Poetry from the Kings' Sagas 2: From c.1036 to c.1300, I: Poetry by Named Skalds c.1035–1105; II: Poetry by Named Skalds c.1105–1300 and Anonymous Poetry." *Medium Aevum* 79.2 (November 2010) 350–51.
Omar, A. Rashied. "Embracing the "Other" as an Extension of the Self: Muslim Reflections on the Epistle to the Hebrews 13:2." *Anglican Theological Review* 91.3 (Summer 2009) 433–41.
Orden de Santiago, and Enrique Gallego Blanco. *The Rule of the Spanish Military Order of St. James 1170–1493: Latin and Spanish Texts*. Leiden: Brill, 1971.
Ossorio, Aurora Salvatierra. "Shem Tov ibn Falaquera, from Logic to Ethics: A Redefinition of Poetry in the Thirteenth Century." *Comparative Literature Studies* 45.2 (2008) 165–81.
Pankhurst, Reza. "Muslim Contestations over Religion and the State in the Middle East." *Political Theology* 11.6 (December 2010) 826–45.
Payne, Stanley G. *Spanish Catholicism: An Historical Overview*. Madison, WI: University of Wisconsin Press, 1984.
Pardo Pastor, Jordi. "Diálogo Interreligioso en la Edad Media Hispánica: Consideraciones Históricas a Partir del Concilio Vaticano II." *Estudios Eclesiásticos* 79.309 (April 2004) 217–60.
Peers, Edgar Allison. *Art of Contemplation*. London: Macmillan, 1925.

———. *Fool of Love*. London: SCM, 1946.
———. *The Mystics of Spain*. London: Allen and Unwin, 1951.
———. *Ramon Lull: A Biography*. London: Society for Promoting Christian Knowledge, 1929.
Peers, E. Allison. "Ramon Lull and the World of Today." *Hispania* 11.6 (1928) 459–67.
Petry, Ray C. *Late Medieval Mysticism*. London: SCM, 1957.
Pindel-Buchel, Theodor. "The Relationship between the Epistemologies of Ramon Lull and Nicholas of Cusa." *American Catholic Philosophical Quarterly* 64.1 (1990) 73–87.
Powell, Jatnes M. "St. Francis of Assisi's Way of Peace." *Medieval Encounters* 13.2 (July 2007) 271–80.
Powers, James F. "Frontier Municipal Baths and Social Interaction in Thirteenth-Century Spain." *The American Historical Review* 84.3 (June 1979) 649–67.
Prior, Laurence P. "Francis of Assisi and a Cosmic Spirituality." *Religion & Theology* 18.1/2 (January 2011) 173–94.
Rahman, Abdur. "Islam Regards Women as Spiritual and Intellectual Equals of Men." *Hamdard Islamicus* 31.3 (July 2008) 88–91.
Rampling, Jennifer M. "Establishing the Canon: George Ripley and his Alchemical Sources." *Ambix* 55.3 (November 2008) 189–208.
Rashdall, Hastings, and F. M. Powicke. *The Universities of Europe in the Middle Ages*. London: Oxford University Press, 1936.
Rhodes, Ron. *Reasoning from the Scriptures with the Muslims*. Eugene, OR: Harvest House, 2002.
Robson, Michael J. P., ed. *The Cambridge Companion to Francis of Assisi*. Cambridge: Cambridge University Press, 2012.
Robinson, Cynthia. "Trees of Love, Trees of Knowledge: Toward the Definition of a Cross-Confessional Current in Late Medieval Iberian Spirituality." *Medieval Encounters* 12.3 (November 2006) 388–435.
Robinson, Scott. "To Go among the Saracens." *Cross Currents* 56.3 (Fall 2006) 413–23.
Rodriguez, Jarbel. *Captives and Their Saviors in the Medieval Crown of Aragon*. Washington, DC: Catholic University of America Press, 2007.
———. *Muslim and Christian Contact in the Middle Ages: A Reader*. Toronto, University of Toronto Press, 2015.
Rohr, Richard, Andreas Richard, and Peter Heineqq. *The Enneagram: A Christian Perspective*. New York: Crossroad, 2001.
Romero Carrasquillo, Francisco. "Intellectual Elitism and the Need for Faith in Maimonides and Aquinas." *Anuario Filosófico* 48.1 (March 2015) 79–102.
Roth, Pinchas. "Regional Boundaries and Medieval Halakhah: Rabbinic Responsa from Catalonia to Southern France in the Thirteenth and Fourteenth Centuries." *Jewish Quarterly Review* 105.1 (Winter 2015) 72–98.
Rubenstein, Richard E. *Aristotle's Children: How Christians, Muslims, and Jews Rediscovered Ancient Wisdom and Illuminated the Dark Ages*. Orlando: Harcourt, 2003.
Ruiz Simón, Josep Maria. "El Joc de Ramon Llull i la Significació de l'Art General." *Journal Ars Brevis* 2 (1998) 55–65.
———. "Per Comprendre l'Art de Ramon Llull. L'aportació d'Anthony Bonner." *Journal Els Marges* 87 (2009) 65–72.

Ruiz Simon, Josep M., and Albert Soler Llopart. "Ramon Llull in His Historical Context." *Catalan Historical Review* No.1 (2008) 47–61.

Rustom, Mohammed. "Approaching Mullā Ṣadrā as Scriptural Exegete: A Survey of Scholarship on His Quranic Works." *Comparative Islamic Studies* 4.1/2 (June 2008) 75–96.

Saint Bonaventure of Bagnoregio. *Journey of the Mind of God*. Grand Rapids: Christian Classic Ethereal Library, 2013.

Sanaullah, Mohammad. "Andalusian Seers, Sufi-Cristiano and the Cultismo: Prologue on a Shared Legacy of Scholastic Mysticism and Poetry." *Hamdard Islamicus* 30.4 (October 2007) 45–66.

Samir, Khalil, and Jørgen S. Nielsen. *Christian Arabic apologetics during the Abbasid period, 750–1258*. Leiden: E.J. Brill, 1994.

Scarpelly Cory, Therese. "The Liber De Causis, Avicenna, and Aquinas's Turn to Phantasms." *Tópicos: Revista de Filosofía* 45 (December 2013) 129–62.

Schmidt, Martin Anton. "Thomas Aquinas and Raymundus Lullus." *Church History* 29.2 (1960) 123–40.

Schoedinger, Andrew B. *Readings in Medieval Philosophy*. New York: Oxford University Press, 1996.

Selart, Anti. "Popes and Livonia in the First Half of the Thirteenth Century: Means and Chances to Shape the Periphery." *Catholic Historical Review* 100.3 (Summer 2014) 437–58.

Şenocak, Neslihan. "The Franciscan Order and Natural Philosophy in the Thirteenth Century: A Relationship Redefined." *Ecotheology: Journal of Religion, Nature & the Environment* 7.2 (January 2003) 113–25.

Shapiro, Herman. *Medieval Philosophy: Selected Readings from Augustine to Buridan*. New York: Modern Library, 1964.

Shahzad, Qaiser. "Accommodating Trinity: A Brief Note on Ibn ʿArabī's Views." *Journal of Ecumenical Studies* 48.1 (Winter 2013) 114–20.

Sharp, Tristan. "Tractatvs De Confessione "Activvs Contemplativo: A Thirteenth-Century Guide to Confession for Monks." *Mediaeval Studies* 76 (January 2014) 1–56.

Sire, James W. *Apologetics beyond Reason: Why Seeing Really Is Believing*. Downers Grove, IL: Intervarsity, 2014.

Skopalová, Eva. "The Mantegna Tarocchi and the View of the World in Northern Italy in the 15th Century." *Umeni/Art* 62.6 (November 2014) 502–15.

Smith, Damian J. *Crusade, Heresy and Inquisition in the Lands of the Crown of Aragon, c. 1167–1276*. Boston: Brill, 2010.

Sokolow, Moshe. "Knowledge and Action, Reason and Habit, in Jewish and Muslim Philosophies of Education." *Journal of Research on Christian Education* 22.1 (January 2013) 21–29.

Spevack, Aaron. "Apples and Oranges: The Logic of the Early and Later Arabic Logicians." *Islamic Law & Society* 17.2 (May 2010) 159–84.

Spruyt, Joke. "The 'Forma-Materia' Device in Thirteenth-Century Logic and Semantics." *Vivarium* 41.1 (2003) 1–46.

Stillman, Yedida Kalfon, and Norman A. Stillman. *From Iberia to Diaspora: Studies in Sephardic History and Culture*. Leiden: Brill, 1999.

Stumpf, Samuel Enoch. *Socrates to Sartre: A History of Philosophy*. New York: McGraw Hill, 1999.

Sweeney, Michael. "Greek Essence And Islamic Tolerance: Al-Farabi, Al-Ghazali, Ibn Rush'd." *Review of Metaphysics* 65.1 (September 2011) 41–61.

Sweeny, Michael J. "Philosophy and Jihād: Al-Fārābī on Compulsion to Happiness." *Review of Metaphysics* 60.3 (March 2007) 543–72.

Szarmach, Paul E. *An Introduction to the Medieval Mystics of Europe: Fourteen Original Essays.* Albany: State University of New York Press, 1984.

Tartakoff, Paola. *Middle Ages Series: Between Christian and Jew: Conversion and Inquisition in the Crown of Aragon, 1250–1391.* Philadelphia: University of Pennsylvania Press, 2012.

Tavasolli, Sasan, and Kevin Higgins. "The Ethics of Qur'an Interpretation in Muslim Evangelism and Insider Movements." *Evangelical Review of Theology* 37.4 (October 2013) 321–34.

Taylor, Richard C. "Averroes on the Ontology of the Human Soul." *The Muslim World* 102S.3–4 (July 2012) 580–96.

———. "Critical eds of Averroes' Middle Commentaries, review of 3 Books." *The Muslim World* 75.3–4 (July 1985) 188–89.

———. "Ibn Rushd/Averroes and 'Islamic' Rationalism." *Medieval Encounters* 15.2–4 (December 2009) 225–35.

Tolan, John. "Saracen Philosophers Secretly Deride Islam." *Medieval Encounters* 8.2/3 (2002) 184–208.

Troeger, Eberhard. "The Concept of Salvation in the Christian-Muslim Encounter: A Response." *Direction* 23.1 (1994) 17–21.

Truglia, Craig. "Al-Ghazali and Giovanni Pico Della Mirandola on the Question of Human Freedom and the Chain of Being." *Philosophy East & West* 60.2 (April 2010) 143–66.

Turberville, Arthur Stanley. *The Spanish Inquisition.* Hamden, CT: Archon, 1968.

Urban, William. "The Forgotten Crusaders: Poland and the Crusader Movement in the Twelfth and Thirteenth Centuries." *The Catholic Historical Review* 3 (2013) 545–48.

Vagelpohl, Uwe. "The Prior Analytics in the Syriac and Arabic tradition." *Vivarium* 48.1/2 (March 2010) 134–58.

Valenzuela, Claudia. "The Faith of the Saracens: Forms of Knowledge of Islam in the Christian Kingdoms of the Iberian Peninsula until the 12th Century." *Millennium* 10 (2013) 311–30.

Vega, Amador. *Ramon LLull and the Secret of Life.* New York: Crossroad, 2002.

Vella, John A. *Aristotle: A Guide for the Perplexed.* London; New York: Continuum, 2008.

Watson, A J. "Nothing to Gain from the Forest?: Ramon Llull's Radical Monotheism and Islamic Thought." *Missiology* 37.4 (October 2009) 555–70.

Waugh, Scott L., and Peter D. Diehl. *Christendom and Its Discontents: Exclusion, Persecution, and Rebellion, 1000–1500.* Cambridge, England: Cambridge University Press, 1996.

Weiler, Antonius Gerardus. "The Requirements of the Pastor Bonus in the Late Middle Ages." *Nederlands Archief Voor Kerkgeschiedenis* 83.1 (2003) 57–83.

Whalen, B. E. "Corresponding with Infidels: Rome, the Almohads, and the Christians of Thirteenth-Century Morocco." *Journal of Medieval and Early Modern Studies* 41.3 (2011) 487–514.

Wilson, H. S. "Salvation in World Religions." *Mission Studies* 19.1–2 (January 2002) 108–36.

Wilson, Robin. "Early European Mathematics." *Mathematical Intelligencer* 36.1 (February 2014) 82.
White, James R. *The Forgotten Trinity: Recovering the Heart of the Christian Belief.* Minneapolis: Bethany House, 1998.
Yates, Frances A. "The Art of Ramon Lull: An Approach to It through Lull's Theory of the Elements." *Journal of the Warburg and Courtauld Institutes* 17.1 (1954) 115–73.
———. "Ramon Lull and John Scotus Erigena." *Journal of the Warburg and Courtauld Institutes* 23.1/2 (1960) 1–44.
Yucel, Salih. "Muslim-Christian Dialogue: Nostra Aetate and Fethullah Gülen's Philosophy of Dialogue." *Australian E-Journal of Theology* 20.3 (December 2013) 197–206.
Zaldívar, Antonio M. "Patricians' Embrace of the Dominican Convent of St. Catherine in Thirteenth-Century Barcelona." *Medieval Encounters* 18.2/3 (July 2012) 174–206.
Zaleski, Carol, and Philip Zaleski. "Saint Francis, the Catholic Church, and Islam." *Nova Et Vetera* (English ed.) 13.1 (Winter 2015) 39–55.
Zwemer, Samuel Marinus. "Francis of Assisi and Islam." *The Muslim World* 39.4 (October 1949) 247–51.
Zwemer, Samuel M. *Ramon LLull: First Missionary to Moslems*. New York: Funk and Wagnalls, 1902.